# THE FOUNDATIONS OF FEELING GOOD

A Practical Guide to Raising Your Baseline Happiness Through Stoicism, Purpose and Change

## Dominic Byrne

HEMBURY
—BOOKS—

# ABOUT THE AUTHOR

Dominic Byrne writes from the place where despair collides with renewal, where life's hardest struggles can spark profound psychological growth.

When his wife, Louise, became too unwell to write about her cancer journey, Dominic stepped in to continue her story. After her passing, he found healing through words, continuing to share his reflections and discoveries. Writing became both therapy and a compass, guiding him through grief toward self-discovery, resilience and a deeper understanding of happiness.

On this journey, Dominic came to realise that our "set point" for happiness isn't fixed and it can be raised. What began as a heartfelt guide for his youngest sibling gradually evolved into the foundation of his first book, *The Foundations of Feeling Good*.

Based in Sydney, Dominic runs a web design and development business while also raising his two children as a full-time single parent. A former professional athlete, he has rediscovered the discipline, drive and joy of challenge, building a personal framework to support his body, mind and soul. His values are anchored in one clear vision: to live fully and remain active long enough to be a present, supportive grandparent decades from now.

Copyright © Dominic Byrne 2025
First published by Hembury Books in 2025
hemburybooks.com.au
info@hemburybooks.com

Paperback ISBN 9781923517424
Ebook ISBN 9781923517417
Hardback ISBN 9781923517486

The moral right of the author has been asserted.
All rights reserved. No portion of this book may be reproduced in any form without permission from the author and publisher, except as permitted by Australian copyright law.

 A catalogue record for this book is available from the National Library of Australia

**To Noah and Evie**

*Thanks to your mother's beautiful genes — and the steady love of your grandparents, aunts, uncles, cousins and friends — you've grown into the kindest, most respectful, creative, empathetic, fair, and fiercely independent souls I know.*

*Lou's star, and the entire galaxy around it, shines brighter because you're in this world.*

*Every word in this book reflects my love for you.*

**Dad**

# CONTENTS

ABOUT THE AUTHOR ................................................. 3
INTRODUCTION ........................................................ 8
CHAPTER 1 ................................................................ 16
CHAPTER 2 ................................................................ 26
CHAPTER 3 ................................................................ 39
CHAPTER 4 ................................................................ 45
CHAPTER 5 ................................................................ 61
CHAPTER 6 ................................................................ 72
CHAPTER 7 ................................................................ 88
CHAPTER 8 ................................................................ 112
CHAPTER 9 ................................................................ 126
CHAPTER 10 .............................................................. 147
CHAPTER 11 .............................................................. 160
CHAPTER 12 .............................................................. 172
CHAPTER 13 .............................................................. 187
CHAPTER 14 .............................................................. 199
CHAPTER 15 .............................................................. 211
CONCLUSION ........................................................... 221
ACKNOWLEDGEMENTS .......................................... 226

# INTRODUCTION

*"When you arise in the morning, think of what a precious privilege it is to be alive to breathe, think, enjoy, and love."*
— Marcus Aurelius

When I was 45, I wrote down 50 goals I wanted to achieve before my 51st birthday – my 50by50 list. There are several reasons why I did this, and I will explain, but first, let me tell you why you're here.

One of the goals on my 50by50 list was "Write a book."

I lived in the fast lane from my teenage years until my mid-forties. I worked hard during this time. I studied my way through university, was a professional athlete for four years, built my own business, got married and started a family. But, holy shit, did I party.

For close to 30 years of my life, I wouldn't have been out of place if I had been seen with John Daley, Charlie Sheen and Lindsay Lohan in their prime party days. My childhood and school years were also full of wacky adventures. I have some crazy stories to tell, and I always thought a book of legendary tales would be enjoyable to publish. I even mapped out some fun, thrilling chapters of comical yarns that would form the foundation of my book.

When I was 39 and my children were five and three, my wife, Louise, was diagnosed with breast cancer. Eighteen months after her diagnosis, Louise would be dead.

Louise died in my arms in a hospital bed in Germany, her tiny body riddled with tumours. I returned home from Frankfurt to Sydney with our beautiful babies and an empty seat beside us on the plane. From this day, my life would take a different direction, and my priorities would shift.

My energy and attention were channelled into finding my feet as a single parent and raising the two beautiful children Louise had gifted me. Through the first few years on my own, I still managed to self-medicate with alcohol and drug binges of epic proportions. As a full-time single parent, there were fewer windows of opportunity to party, but when that window opened, I certainly took advantage of it.

After three years of being a widower and on my own, I entered into a relationship that fell apart as soon as it started. This was the catalyst that sent me into a spin. I got into the deepest rut and wallowed in so much despair that I barely functioned. Many mornings, after dropping the kids off at school, I would collapse back into bed in a foetal position and stare at the wall, motionless, mustering any scarce energy to get moving for the day and do the bare minimum so my business wouldn't implode. Without the responsibility of caring for Noah and Evie, I hate to think where the lowest point would have landed.

When my depressive state and emotional turmoil bled into my physical appearance, and people were asking questions about my welfare, I knew I had to make a change. I constructed a one-page plan and put the skerricks of effort I had left into crawling my way out of the trench that I emotionally resided in.

During this period of focused recovery, I was gifted two books: one by my sister and one by my dad. My sister handed me a transformative guide that explores the power of releasing attachments and surrendering to the flow of life for greater emotional freedom. My dad gave me a book based on a 2,000-year-old philosophical school of thought that emphasises rationality, virtue and self-discipline to achieve inner tranquillity and resilience in the face of external circumstances.

I hadn't read a book in over a decade, and never one centred around self-help and guidance. These two books aided my emotional recovery and sent me on a crusade to read dozens more books and embark on a healing journey. The momentum and thirst for more knowledge sent me on a pursuit to achieve a state of psychological stability and composure that was undisturbed by the exposure to emotions or pain that would have previously unbalanced me. In the proceeding chapters, I will tease apart multiple books I have combined with my experiences to demonstrate how they helped me—and will help you.

While hitting rock bottom was the catalyst for wellness, the truth is, if my happiness were charted against a horizontal line in the middle from the age of 20 to 45, it would look something like this.

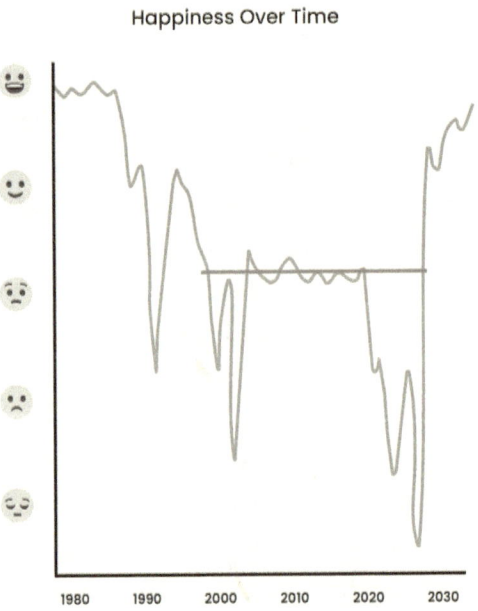

For half of my life, I hovered around or even below the line of contentment. I functioned well—had fun, smiled and laughed—but beneath it all, happiness often felt diluted by the weight of life.

Life isn't easy. It throws us daily challenges, unexpected turns, and moments of adversity. Time moves quickly—minutes into hours, days into years—and with it comes constant change. Societal pressures, family expectations and our own inner critics can create a sense of inadequacy. Mental health struggles, like anxiety, depression or unresolved trauma, can make even the most ordinary tasks feel overwhelming. Relationships, too—while capable of bringing joy—can also bring conflict, misunderstandings and painful loss. At times, life can feel relentlessly heavy.

My internal dialogue often echoed the same thoughts: "This whole living thing is hard. Why am I here? What's the point of all this? I'd rather not be here." While these weren't typically suicidal thoughts, I won't pretend they never touched the edges of that darkness during my lowest moments. More often, it wasn't a desire to die—it was simply not wanting to exist. Life felt like it demanded more effort than the reward it offered. And I know I'm not alone in feeling that way.

But, through time, introspection and hard work, I discovered something powerful: the happiness "set point" is not immovable. I had once accepted that it was fixed. Now I had worked my way through it and beyond it.

The happiness set point refers to the idea that each of us has a genetically influenced baseline level of happiness. It may rise or fall with life events, but eventually, we return to this personal default setting. However, in reflecting on my own journey—especially those times when I felt like life required more than it gave—I realised something important: it wasn't that happiness was unreachable; I was just investing energy in the wrong places.

So, I asked bigger questions: What is happiness? Am I happy?

Can my set point be shifted—and how? What emotional states do I return to after highs and lows? Do I lean towards optimism, or am I weighed down? What habits fuel my wellbeing and which ones drain it? What are my values? What is the best version of me?

Eventually, I learnt this truth: happiness cannot be chased directly. It emerges; a by-product of consistent, meaningful habits that nourish the mind, body and relationships. The practices that elevated and sustained my happiness were not expensive or exclusive. In fact, they were freely available, simple and abundant.

True fulfilment doesn't come from obsessively pursuing happiness. It comes when you focus on what's meaningful—growth, connection, purpose. Happiness then becomes the natural outcome.

But make no mistake: elevating your baseline happiness takes serious work. It requires building a personal framework—one that aligns with your values and supports your body, mind and soul. You must seek or create a sense of purpose and align your daily actions with it. You must show up for yourself. Contributing to something greater than yourself or deeply caring for others can create profound shifts in your sense of meaning and joy.

When you don't live up to your potential—when you ignore your own capacity to grow—you may feel the burden of frustration, guilt and regret. You begin to question your worth, lose motivation and sink into cycles of self-doubt. These feelings compound, becoming barriers to growth and joy.

In building my own framework, I wanted to share what was working with my youngest sibling, who was facing challenges that kept her from fully flourishing. I wrote a guide for her. Alisha's feedback was so heartfelt and encouraging that I began sharing it with more friends and family. As the circle widened, and as people began finding healing through these ideas, I knew it was time to share them more broadly.

That's why you're here.

You've probably figured it out by now: this isn't the book you might've expected. It's not a recount of wild escapades, near-death experiences or drunken stupidity, though I've had my fair share of all of that. In fact, this entire project started from a very different place.

Somehow, I've landed on the other side of a paradigm shift. I started in a hollow, hedonistic, self-destructive place—and arrived here. Now, I'm recommending lifestyle and behavioural changes that, if applied consistently, can help close the gap between merely surviving and actually feeling happy.

Here's what you'll gain as you move through the pages of this book:

- What happiness is—from my perspective to yours
- The core of Stoicism and how it supports lasting happiness
- Why continual learning matters—keep the knowledge flowing
- Discipline, discipline, discipline
- The truth about habits—and how to change them
- Alcohol—quit for 12 months, then decide
- Nutrition—because food really is medicine
- Movement—use your body or lose its potential
- Mindfulness—rest your body, mind, and soul
- The magic of early rising—feel the difference
- Post-traumatic growth—rise, and rise again
- Living like a Stoic
- Letting go—clear what blocks your joy
- Finding and working on your purpose
- Stitching it all together—where happiness follows

I'm not a doctor, a dietitian, a psychologist or a personal trainer. I'm a full-time single parent and a self-employed business owner who's just trying to keep all the balls in the air and do life well. I've made plenty of mistakes, but I've also made progress—and that's what this book is really about.

It's never too late to make a change. If you're unhappy, there is a way through. And if you're already happy, why not raise the baseline even higher?

The principles in this book can elevate the quality of your work, your play and your relationships. I've become a happy person, not by luck, but through intentional choices—and you can too. Life is so much more vibrant when you move from "getting by" to "feeling good most of the time."

When you're in a good place, something beautiful happens:
- Music sounds better.
- Colours appear brighter.
- Spring air smells fresher.
- Healthy food tastes incredible.
- A loving touch hits deeper.
- You're more patient, more motivated.
- You make better decisions.
- You sleep well.
- You live wide awake.
- Your awareness sharpens.
- The present moment becomes a refuge, not a blur.
- You feel grounded in a world that often feels chaotic.
- Your perspective shifts, revealing the deeper meaning and connection in everyday life.

Change begins now. The hardest part is starting, but what may feel like turning your life upside down is actually just setting it the right way up.

Feeling good most days is a journey, not a fluke. I found the silver bullet to happiness, but I had to cast the casing, source the primers, mould the projectiles, and learn to aim accurately at life's daily challenges. You'll have to craft your own ammunition too. Each chapter is designed to give you the tools or spark the motivation to do just that.

Creating your own system for happiness is a deeply rewarding process. It's not easy—it demands discipline, focus and heart. But the work is good. And the pay-off is better than you can imagine.

CHAPTER 1

# WHAT HAPPINESS IS, FROM MY PERSPECTIVE TO YOURS

*"The groundwork for all happiness is good health."*
— *Leigh Hunt*

When we inquire about someone's happiness in relation to their performance, daily experience or activity, we refer to a transient form of happiness—a fleeting perspective. You could call it micro-happiness.

Whenever we ask someone if they are happy—happy in a relationship, at work or at home—it is associated with a constant, a more profound life satisfaction in the long term; it's macro-happiness. You can have many positive micro-happiness experiences and subpar macro-happiness. Many people do, and I did.

We are deeply concerned if a loved one has expressed unhappiness based on a "constant" enquiry or observation. Our self-evaluation only requires a little investigation to know if we are not feeling good. When you don't feel good, you may encounter a list of emotions and feelings often associated with unhappiness, including sadness, loneliness, frustration, anger, disappointment, despair, hopelessness, guilt, regret, anxiety, fear, resentment, bitterness, envy, jealousy, grief, stress, agitation, irritability, insecurity and more.

On the flip side, emotions and feelings often associated with being happy include joy, contentment, excitement, love, gratitude, satisfaction, peace, enthusiasm, optimism, pride, amusement, euphoria, relief, delight, cheerfulness, warmth, hopefulness, confidence, serenity and elation. These negative and positive emotions can vary in intensity and may be experienced in combination, contributing to an overall sense of happiness—or lack of it.

These associated emotions and our different perspectives of fleeting or constant happiness produce a mosaic definition. With its myriad interpretations and deeply personal, subjective nature, it is challenging to establish a universal standard for happiness. But it's a subject everyone can relate to, prompting each person to reflect on their unique understanding of it.

When I was more than 60 per cent through this book I had a perspective on what happiness is, but struggled to articulate it. Since I didn't have my definition of happiness, I went on a quest to create one, and then altered the book accordingly.

We each need a definition of happiness. Therefore you have a framework for understanding happiness, because achieving happiness requires self-discipline and moral integrity that can be challenging to maintain.

Austrian psychiatrist and Holocaust survivor Victor Frankel said, "… happiness cannot be pursued; it must ensue, and it only does so as the unintended side-effect of one's dedication to a cause greater than oneself or as the by-product of one's surrender to a person other than oneself. Happiness must happen, and the same holds for success: you must let it happen by not caring about it."

Frankl emphasised that happiness is not a goal that can be achieved directly. Instead, it comes as a natural outcome of dedicating oneself to meaningful pursuits or caring deeply for others. Frankl suggests that true fulfilment arises not from chasing happiness, but from focusing on something greater than yourself—a cause, a purpose, or a connection with others. If you immerse yourself in a purpose without obsessing over personal happiness, happiness will naturally follow.

Friedrich Nietzsche, a 19th-century German philosopher, had a complex and often counterintuitive view of happiness. Unlike many thinkers who equate happiness with comfort, pleasure or peace, Nietzsche associated true happiness with struggle, growth and the pursuit of meaning, even through suffering. In Nietzsche's view, happiness is not about avoiding pain, but about embracing life fully, including its hardships. He believed that joy comes from overcoming difficulties and from the feeling of power that arises when we face challenges and grow stronger. One of his most famous lines sums this up: "What does not kill me makes me stronger."

He also linked happiness to the concept of the will to power—the inner drive to grow, to assert oneself and to create. For Nietzsche, happiness was the result of living authentically, pushing beyond conventional morality and affirming life in all its complexity.

Moreover, Nietzsche admired those who could create their own values and live courageously in a world without objective meaning. In this way, happiness was not passive contentment, but an active expression of strength, creativity and self-overcoming. Nietzsche defined happiness not as comfort or ease, but as the deep, often hard-won joy that comes from living boldly, embracing struggle and becoming who you truly are.

Haemin Sunim, the Korean Buddhist monk and author, defines happiness as a state of inner peace, self-acceptance and presence. For him, happiness is something that can be experienced in the present moment, not something to be chased or achieved in the future. He emphasises that we can still be happy while working towards our goals, as happiness isn't far away—it lives in the here and now. A central part of his teaching is the importance of self-compassion: when we stop judging ourselves harshly and begin to accept ourselves as we are, we open the door to inner contentment. Happiness, in his view, also grows from slowing down and appreciating the small, simple joys of life, like a warm drink, a gentle breeze or a shared smile. He highlights the value of love and connection, encouraging us to nurture meaningful relationships and approach life with an open heart. True happiness arises from mindfulness, kindness and the quiet beauty of everyday life rather than in external success or perfection.

Socrates, Plato and Aristotle were significant influences on the Stoics, and the Stoics have been a considerable influence on my version of happiness. Their focus is on a state of flourishing and living well, characterised by fulfilling one's potential and living a life of virtue and reason. It's about stable mental health and mood, characterised by a sense of wellbeing, emotional balance, and a concept of excellence and fulfilling purpose while embodying the highest quality and effectiveness.

I will elaborate on this as we progress through the pages. Still, by practising virtue, maintaining mindfulness, visualising adversity, detaching from externals, developing resilience and cultivating gratitude, we can achieve a state of eudaemonia—a deeply fulfilling and enduring form of happiness. The Stoic path to happiness is a lifelong journey of self-improvement and philosophical reflection.

Influenced by others, like Frankl, Nitzsche, Sunim and the Stoics, I arrived at my definition from a philosophical standpoint because it provides guiding principles and frameworks to help me achieve a balanced and meaningful life. It encourages me to consider the totality of my life, including relationships, personal growth, knowledge, mindfulness, health and contributions to society. It focuses on flourishing and fulfilling one's potential over a lifetime rather than just seeking momentary micro-happiness. The philosophical perspectives I admire link happiness to virtue and ethical living, suggesting that true happiness is intertwined with a morally good life. Emphasising the importance of self-examination and personal growth is crucial for achieving a more profound sense of happiness.

In my research on the definition of happiness and the pursuit of it, I understand that being happy every single day is inherently improbable due to the dynamic nature of human experiences, emotional variability and external circumstances.

Human emotions are inherently fluid and subject to change. The complexity of the human emotional spectrum makes it impossible to sustain a single emotional state, such as happiness, continuously. Emotions are not static; they ebb and flow in response to internal and external factors. This variability is a fundamental aspect of the human experience, allowing us to navigate different situations and adapt to changing circumstances.

External factors significantly influence one's emotional state. Life is replete with challenges, setbacks and uncertainties that can disrupt feelings of happiness. Personal losses, health issues, financial difficulties and interpersonal conflicts are common occurrences that can evoke negative emotions. These experiences are part of the human condition and contribute to emotional diversity. The inevitability of encountering difficult situations makes the idea of perpetual happiness unrealistic.

Humans have a remarkable capacity for psychological adaptation, which can impact the sustainability of happiness. The set point concept I mentioned in the introduction suggests that people tend to return to a baseline level of happiness regardless of positive or negative life changes. For instance, achieving a significant goal or acquiring a desired possession may lead to temporary happiness. Still, over time, people often revert to their pre-existing level of happiness (which I know now can be elevated). This adaptation mechanism highlights the transient nature of happiness and underscores the difficulty of maintaining it consistently.

Expectations and societal pressures can also affect our ability to experience happiness. Contemporary society often emphasises achieving constant happiness, fuelled by portrayals of idealised lives on social media. This creates unrealistic expectations, which can lead to feeling inadequate and dissatisfied when one's life does not measure up. The pressure to be perpetually happy can paradoxically result in increased stress and reduced overall happiness.

Experiencing various emotions, including those perceived as unfavourable, is essential for personal growth and emotional resilience. Negative emotions such as sadness, frustration and anxiety serve essential functions by signalling when something is wrong or needs attention. They encourage introspection, problem-solving and adaptation. Without the full spectrum of emotions, we would lack the depth and understanding to contribute to a meaningful and fulfilling life.

A meaningful and fulfilling life is where my sense of happiness comes from, which is the philosophical lens through which I will write this book. In my opinion, you can regularly feel joy, pleasure and delight and still have a subpar level of happiness.

Focusing on the philosophical perspective of happiness can help us better understand what it means to live a good and fulfilling life. This perspective goes beyond immediate gratification and integrates virtue, personal growth and meaningful living, offering a profound and enduring sense of fulfilment. It encourages us to strive for excellence and contribute positively to society, leading to a richer and more satisfying life.

The philosophical influences I have adopted often advocate for a balanced approach and recognise that excess or deficiency in any area can impact overall wellbeing. The philosophers I follow encourage rational thought and critical analysis, helping us to make informed decisions that lead to lasting happiness and emphasising the importance of finding meaning and purpose, which are crucial to elevating happiness.

And my definition of happiness:

Happiness begins with sound metabolic health, serving as the foundation for overall wellbeing. It is living in alignment with your core values. Happiness is not a fixed destination but an ongoing journey of personal growth. True happiness involves striving for excellence in every interaction, consistently fulfilling your potential with authenticity and integrity. It embodies resilience, remaining steadfast amid external challenges. Happiness is knowing and living your purpose, contributing positively to society, and embracing self-acceptance and inner peace. It is rooted in gratitude for the present moment, fostering a sense of contentment and fulfilment.

While my definition is a continuous journey, and it may change with time, I have learnt that it's only really the beginning. Because if you are healthy in body and mind, flourish, and teach yourself to be grateful, happiness can be everywhere and everything. In the realm of emotions, happiness is the golden thread weaving through the fabric of our lives, illuminating our existence with its warm glow. It's that ineffable sensation, like catching the sunlight in your hands and feeling its gentle warmth seep into your soul.

Imagine consistently waking up to the soft hues of dawn painting the sky and feeling a gentle flutter in your chest as you realise that today holds promises yet to unfold. Your heart dances to the rhythm of anticipation, eager to embrace the adventures ahead. As you step outside, the world seems to shimmer with possibility. Every blade of grass, every whispering breeze, seems to whisper secrets of joy. The air is alive with the melody of birdsong, and the fragrance of flowers dances on the breeze, lifting your spirits higher with every inhalation. You find yourself smiling at the simplest things—the flutter of a bird, the sight of a child walking their dog, the warmth of a stranger's smile. In these moments, happiness is found in the small, fleeting moments that make life beautiful.

It's the feeling of connection, of belonging, as you share laughter with friends or bask in the warmth of familial love. It's the warmth of a hug, the comfort of a shared silence, the knowledge that you are seen and cherished for exactly who you are.

Happiness is the gentle rhythm of contentment, the sense of peace that settles in your soul like a warm, comfortable bed on a chilly night. It's the feeling of being exactly where you're meant to be, of finding solace in the present moment and gratitude for all that you have.

It's the exhilarating adrenaline rush as you chase your dreams and the sense of accomplishment as you reach new heights and overcome obstacles. It's the thrill of discovery, the joy of creation, the satisfaction of knowing that you are living a life true to yourself.

And yet, happiness is also the quiet stillness of a moment paused—a sunset painting the sky in tones of fire, a cup of tea shared with a loved one, or a book that transports you to another world. It's the ability to find beauty in the ordinary, to savour the sweetness of life's simple pleasures.

In the tapestry of human experience, happiness is the thread that binds us, the universal language that transcends borders and cultures. It's a gift we give ourselves and each other, a reminder that even in the darkest times, there is always a glimmer of light waiting to be found.

In our pursuit of happiness, we often chase after fleeting moments of joy—vacations, promotions, social approval or material possessions. While these can offer temporary boosts, true, enduring happiness is more nuanced and deeply rooted in a foundational element: wellness.

As the Dalai Lama says, "Happiness is the highest form of health." Through my journey and reflection, I've come to realise that wellness must come first. It's the scaffold upon which happiness is built. Without a solid base of physical, mental, emotional and spiritual health, happiness becomes unstable, fragile and transient. But when wellness is prioritised, happiness becomes a steady, enduring baseline that supports us through life's inevitable ups and downs.

For me, when the elements that make up this book are in harmony, they create a resilient foundation that underpins my macro-level happiness. Without wellness, happiness can become superficial or fleeting, dependent on external circumstances rather than internal stability. Prioritising wellness allows me to develop a strong sense of self-awareness, respond thoughtfully rather than react impulsively, cultivate sustainable habits that support long-term happiness and see happiness as a tool for self-care and reflection, not just a fleeting emotion.

Happiness is a beautiful state, but it's not something to chase directly. Instead, focus on building wellness—your personalised scaffolding—that supports a steady, resilient baseline of happiness. By nurturing your mind, body and spirit, you create a life where happiness is not an elusive goal but a natural by-product of a balanced, well-lived life.

## REMEMBER THIS

Wellness is a journey. Invest in it daily, tailor it to your unique needs, and watch how happiness becomes a more enduring, enriching part of your life. After all, true happiness flows from a foundation of genuine wellness.

Stop and think about what happiness means to you. This is important because you must take control of your story and become the creator of your life. My book is relevant regardless of your definition, as it will be a catalyst in the design and architecture of the scaffolding that will become your system to increase the base levels of your definition of happiness. Create and curate your version of happiness, and write it down in your journal. If you don't have one, start one today. "My definition of happiness" can be the first page.

So, let's get disciplined from this day on, with the overarching aim of organically embracing happiness in all its forms—in the laughter that fills our hearts, the love that surrounds us and the beauty that graces our world.

CHAPTER 2

# WHAT STOICISM IS AND HOW IT RELATES TO BEING HAPPY

*"Man is disturbed not by things, but by the views he takes of them."*
— *Epictetus*

I mentioned a life-changing book in the introduction, a book my dad gifted to me on Christmas Day 2022. It is based on a 2,000-year-old philosophical school of thought that emphasises rationality, virtue and self-discipline to achieve inner tranquillity and resilience in the face of external circumstances. That philosophy is Stoicism, and the book my dad gave me is *Reasons Not to Worry* by Brigid Delaney.

Suppose the first book I read had been one of the ancient publications on Stoicism, like Seneca's *A Short Life*, Epictetus's *Discourses*, or Marcus Aurelius's *Meditations*. I may not have immediately fallen in love with the philosophy. But luckily I arrived through Delaney's engaging and accessible writing style, as she distilled the ancient wisdom into practical advice without losing the essence of Stoic thought. Her modern interpretations of classical ideas are presented with clarity and relevance, making it easier to apply these concepts to my daily life more effectively. Whether you are new to Stoicism or a seasoned practitioner, *Reasons Not to Worry* provides valuable insights that resonate deeply.

This book you are reading now is littered with Stoic ideas and influences. I've read more than 20 books on the subject and have applied the concepts I learnt with positive results.

If you're new to Stoicism and find the philosophy intriguing, it's likely to ignite a curiosity that will lead you to delve deeper into the literature and learn more about it. In the following chapters I will only scratch the surface of the surviving history and the Stoic philosophers who created, developed and taught it.

People like Socrates, Plato, Aristotle, Zeno, Epictetus, Seneca and Aurelius were far brighter than I will ever be. Still, their wisdom is what we, as students, can absorb and apply to become better human beings, elevate our happiness, and perhaps even flourish.

Before I explain Stoicism, be aware that being stoic is only distantly related to being a Stoic. The first is a common behaviour, while the second is a philosophical practice. When someone is described as stoic (with a lower-case s), it usually refers to a demeanour characterised by emotional restraint. A stoic person appears composed and unaffected by strong emotions like joy, anger or sadness, often as a way of coping with difficult situations. This is more about behaviour—a "stiff upper lip" approach showing little outward expression of emotions, especially in challenging moments.

On the other hand, being a Stoic (with a capital S) refers to following the philosophy of Stoicism. The origin of the word has no relation to lower case stoic.

If I were to explain Stoicism in one sentence, it would be: We have a purpose: to be the best human we can be.

Let me explain Stoicism in a paragraph, and then we will tease it apart. Founded by Zeno of Citium, Stoicism is a 2,000-year-old philosophy that started in Greece and spread to Rome. It's a practical methodology for seeking wisdom in life. We don't react to events; we react to our judgements about them, which are up to us. In other words, we don't control what happens to us, but we do control how we respond to it. Everything that happens to us in life is an opportunity to respond with what the philosophy calls virtue. Virtue comprises four intertwined sources: courage, justice, temperance and wisdom. Living with virtue is about being the best possible human being, having an excellent inner guiding spirit, and making good choices.

Read that paragraph again, and let it sink in. It's good, huh?

Stoicism offers timeless wisdom for cultivating resilience, virtue and inner peace. By understanding its history, key figures, principles and modern applications, we can integrate Stoic philosophy into our lives, making us more thoughtful, disciplined and prepared for life's inevitable challenges.

Stoicism emphasises living in harmony with reason, accepting that life is impermanent and that death, loss and change are inevitable. This acceptance fosters tranquillity even in difficult times, bringing a sense of contentment and fulfilment. Stoics focus on the present moment, believing that happiness can be found in the here and now, rather than being deferred until we reach some future achievement. Dwelling on the past or worrying about the future only distracts from the present, which is the only time we truly have.

From a Stoic perspective, suffering is a natural part of life but does not have to diminish happiness. Instead, it can be an opportunity for personal growth and the practice of virtue. Stoics transform adversity into a source of resilience and self-improvement, seeing challenges as part of life's unfolding rather than obstacles to be avoided. Ultimately, Stoicism teaches that true happiness comes from cultivating inner virtues, controlling one's reactions to external events, and living in alignment with reason, leading to peace and contentment regardless of life's circumstances.

I've observed that people are initially drawn to Stoicism because of its psychological benefits. At the beginning of their Stoic journey, most are eager to know what it could do for them. This was me to a tee, as I was attracted to managing my emotions, being disciplined, courageous and more balanced. This is likely what you want, too. This self-centred version of Stoicism is terrific; it helped me, and it will help you.

You will eventually find a more profound message if you keep learning about Stoicism and practising what it offers. I hope you become interested in the philosophy's social aspects, its emphasis on our responsibility to others, and the importance of working for the common welfare of humankind. I will revisit this aspect of Stoicism in Chapter 13, as I believe in the importance of doing things that make the world a better place if we want to live a significant and fulfilled life. This part of Stoicism forms big intentions for me.

But let's now talk about the first part: the foundation of Stoicism as an essential practice, differentiating between what we can change and what we can't and the idea that we should not worry about things beyond our control.

If I was to draw a line through the middle of the page and ask you to write what is within your life's complete control above the line and what is not below, what would you detail above the line?

## DICHOTOMY OF CONTROL

**Within our control?**

**Beyond our control?**

The Stoics call this the Dichotomy of Control—distinguishing between the things over which we have complete control and the things over which we have no control. The answer seen through the Stoic lens will show that there isn't much above the line.

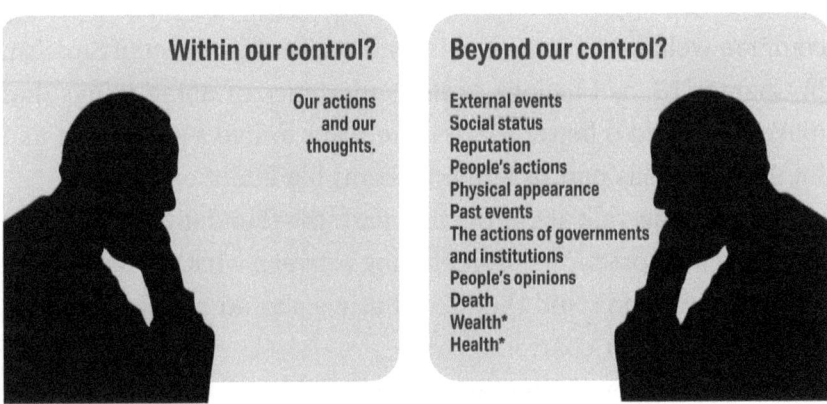

## WHAT CAN WE CONTROL

**Within our control?**
Our actions and our thoughts.

**Beyond our control?**
External events
Social status
Reputation
People's actions
Physical appearance
Past events
The actions of governments and institutions
People's opinions
Death
Wealth*
Health*

We cannot control other people's actions, opinions or behaviours, nor can we control external events like natural disasters, economic downturns or accidents. The past is also beyond our influence, as it cannot be changed. While we can make choices to care for our bodies, certain aspects of our physical appearance and health, such as genetics, aging and illnesses, are out of our control.

Social status and reputation are similarly beyond our full control, as they depend on how others perceive us. The actions of governments, institutions and other organisations are also outside our influence, unless we decide to be part of the organisation. Additionally, the passage of time, natural laws, cosmic events and the basic nature of reality are things we cannot alter. Death, too, is an inevitable part of life that we cannot change.

While we might influence others' emotions and reactions, we cannot control them entirely. The circumstances of our birth, such as where we are born and the socioeconomic conditions we are born into, are beyond our control. Finally, fortune and chance—those random occurrences and strokes of luck or misfortune—are also not something we can dictate. Stoicism teaches that by recognising these limitations and focusing instead on what we can control—our own thoughts, choices and actions—we disconnect from an unwinnable battle and we will be much happier and able to lead a more virtuous life. By focusing on what we can control, we reduce anxiety and frustration. Happiness becomes the result of mastering our responses to life rather than trying to shape the external world.

My favourite part of Stoicism is the concept that translates to virtue or, more simply put, excellence. This idea represents the highest quality that one can achieve, fulfilling one's potential as a rational being. It is striving to maintain the best possible state of one's character by acting virtuously in all situations, regardless of external circumstances. It's a life with rationality and ethical principles, rather than one driven by emotions or societal pressures. It's a continuous practice of self-improvement and learning, requiring constant effort and self-reflection to ensure that one's actions remain aligned with these virtues.

This is where the cardinal virtues come into play: Courage, Justice, Temperance and Wisdom.

**Courage** means having the ability to sustain physical or mental effort over a prolonged period, especially in challenging or demanding situations. It's a strong belief in one's abilities, qualities or judgement, which enable one to act decisively and assertively. It's noble ideals, principles or aspirations, often characterised by a sense of moral integrity and a commitment to acting with honour. It's exhibiting a positive, upbeat attitude and a willingness to spread joy and optimism, often contributing to a pleasant and encouraging atmosphere. It's a diligent and hardworking attitude, consistently applying effort and persistence to achieve goals and complete tasks.

**Justice** is exhibiting deep respect and devotion characterised by morality. It means being truthful and transparent in one's words and actions, consistently adhering to principles of integrity. It means ensuring fairness by providing everyone with equal opportunities and addressing individual needs and circumstances to achieve balanced outcomes. It's engaging in transactions or interactions with honesty, integrity and respect for all parties involved, ensuring that no one is unfairly disadvantaged.

**Temperance** (or moderation) means having the ability to consistently adhere to standards, or self-imposed goals, demonstrating self-control and commitment in one's actions. Exhibiting appropriate and respectful behaviour, appearance or manners that align with your expectations. It means always demonstrating a humble view of one's own achievements or qualities and avoiding excessive pride or self-promotion and, most importantly, it's being able to regulate one's emotions, impulses and behaviours in order to achieve long-term goals and maintain personal discipline.

**Wisdom** is the ability to make sound judgements and decisions based on practical reasoning and awareness. It means being skilled at analysing and assessing situations or problems accurately, often with a focus on strategic planning. It is being able to think and respond rapidly and intelligently, often with cleverness or humour, especially in challenging or unexpected situations. It is the ability to make careful and responsible decisions, especially by exercising good judgement and maintaining confidentiality in sensitive situations. It is to effectively solve problems and adapt to new or difficult situations by using creativity, ingenuity and available resources.

If you and I consistently acted with courage, justice, temperance and wisdom in every interaction and at each decision point, it would deeply influence our lives, relationships and the broader world.

If we acted with courage, we would take action on our principles, challenge injustices, and embrace personal growth despite discomfort or fear. We would develop a stronger sense of integrity and purpose. Our courage would inspire others to be brave and authentic. We would foster an environment where people feel safe to speak their minds and stand up for their values, creating a culture of empowerment. A world guided by courage would see more people acting to right wrongs and defend truth. Social progress would be fuelled by individuals willing to step out of their comfort zones to challenge the status quo.

If we acted with justice, we would approach life with a strong moral compass, treating others equitably and advocating for fairness. Our decisions would be grounded in respect for the dignity and rights of others. We would create relationships based on trust, as others would know we will treat them fairly. People would feel valued, respected and understood. If justice became a guiding principle, societies would move towards greater equality and inclusion. Social systems would be fairer, and there would be less exploitation and oppression, leading to more harmonious coexistence.

If we acted with temperance, or self-control, we would live in moderation, leading to healthier lifestyles, more balanced relationships and greater mental clarity. Emotional regulation would enable us to avoid extremes like indulgence, anger or rashness. We would cultivate deeper, more stable connections. By not overreacting or being excessive in any area, our interactions would be marked by patience, understanding and respect. A temperate world would have less conflict, waste and excess. Resource consumption would be more balanced, and societies would be less prone to the destructive cycles of greed, addiction and impulsive actions.

If we acted with wisdom, we would make well-considered decisions, avoiding rash actions and balancing long-term benefits against short-term temptations. Our lives would be more balanced and we would have fewer regrets. Others would benefit from our measured and thoughtful responses. Relationships would be nurtured through careful listening and well-informed actions, leading to more harmony and less conflict. A wise world would focus on sustainable solutions to problems. Decisions would be made with a deep consideration of the future, reducing impulsive, short-term actions that cause harm, whether to the environment, economy or social systems.

Be motivated by the prospect of harnessing a life lead by these virtues and the personal fulfilment, peace of mind and ethical clarity you would acquire. Our character would be strengthened, and we would navigate life's challenges with resilience and grace. The people around us would experience more trustworthy, compassionate and supportive relationships. We would be positive examples, encouraging others to also act virtuously, creating a ripple effect of moral behaviour.

A society grounded in these virtues would be one of harmony, fairness, sustainability and mutual respect. Conflict would reduce, cooperation would increase, and human progress would be more aligned with the common good rather than individual gain. All our interactions would lead to personal growth, more fulfilling relationships and a fairer, more balanced world. While perfection in this endeavour might not be possible, striving towards it would continually push humanity towards greater ethical and societal harmony.

Virtue, encompassing courage, justice, wisdom and temperance, is considered the only true good in Stoicism. External pleasures, wealth or social status are "indifferent"—neither inherently good nor bad. Stoics believe that living virtuously—acting with integrity, rationality and kindness—is the key to lasting happiness, as it is an internal state that is independent of external conditions. They also teach us that negative emotions like anger, fear and envy stem from incorrect judgements or desires for things outside our control. By cultivating a rational mind and practising mindfulness, Stoics learn to overcome these emotions, leading to greater emotional resilience and deeper happiness.

Becoming a student of the philosophy and practising Stoicism has been a transformative journey, one that has not only improved my life, but has also elevated my happiness in ways I never imagined. In a world full of unpredictability, Stoicism has provided me with a steadier foundation—a philosophy rooted in resilience, acceptance and inner peace.

I am quickly learning to distinguish between what is within my power and what is not. This simple yet profound shift in perspective freed me from unnecessary stress and anxiety. Instead of lamenting uncontrollable events, I am now focusing my energy on my own actions, responses and mindset. With this new-found clarity, I no longer feel burdened by external circumstances, but empowered by my ability to navigate them with composure.

Instead of fearing loss, I often contemplate it, appreciating the present moment even more. By envisioning challenges, I continue to grow more prepared for adversity, making me less susceptible to frustration and disappointment. This practice has cultivated a deep sense of gratitude, as I recognise the fleeting nature of life and cherish what I have with greater intensity.

The wisdom of Stoic thinkers like Marcus Aurelius, Seneca and Epictetus also instilled in me the importance of virtue. I have started measuring success not by my external achievements but by the quality of my character. Courage, justice, temperance and wisdom are key components in my guiding principles. This shift has led me to more fulfilling relationships, a greater sense of purpose, and a genuine alignment with my core values.

Perhaps the most surprising transformation has been my relationship with emotions. Stoicism is often misinterpreted as a call to suppress feelings (I think this comes with the connection to being stoic with a lower case s), but in reality, it teaches mastery over them. For most situations (although the tougher ones are still hard to apply virtue to), I no longer let anger, fear or frustration dictate my actions. Instead, I observe these emotions, acknowledge them, and respond with reasoned judgement rather than impulsive reaction. The result? A more harmonious and emotionally balanced life.

Stoicism has become my anchor in these turbulent times, a guiding philosophy that empowers me to live with intention, resilience and profound contentment. By embracing its principles, I have discovered that true happiness is not found in fleeting pleasures or external validations, but in cultivating a mind that is steady, wise and free. Life is full of unexpected challenges, setbacks and emotional turmoil. This philosophy shifted my perspective and transformed the way I approach life. What I learnt from Stoicism has not only helped me find peace, but has also empowered me to navigate life with resilience and clarity.

****

I now have you at the end of Chapter 2. Thanks for coming on this journey so far. In Chapter 1 I asked you to create and curate your version of happiness, and write it down in your journal. I have another request for you. While I will guide you on living like a Stoic later in the book, let's start doing these three things today so we can make an immediate start.

First, practice The View from Above, a perspective-shifting

exercise. Once a day, visualise yourself from a bird's-eye view, then zoom out further—your city, country, and even the planet. This helps you detach from daily stress and reminds you how small most problems really are in the grand scheme of life. By seeing yourself as just one part of a vast universe, you cultivate humility and gratitude.

Next, incorporate Negative Visualisation (*premeditatio malorum*) into your morning routine. Reflect on potential obstacles or misfortunes that could arise in your day—losing something valuable, facing rejection or encountering unexpected challenges. By imagining these scenarios and accepting them as possibilities, you prepare yourself mentally and emotionally, reducing the shock if they do occur. This practice strengthens resilience and helps you face difficulties with greater composure.

Finally, apply the Dichotomy of Control, a core Stoic principle I have focused on in this chapter. Throughout the day, whenever you feel frustration or anxiety, ask yourself: Is this within my control? If the answer is yes, focus on taking rational, constructive action. If it's no, remind yourself that worrying won't change the outcome and practice letting it go. Surrender the actions of others, external events and the past, and free yourself from the things that can't be changed. By consistently directing your energy only towards what you can influence, you reduce stress and avoid unnecessary frustration.

## REMEMBER THIS

By focusing on your actions, decisions and attitudes with virtuous wisdom, courage, justice and temperance, you can move towards being the best version of yourself. When you start becoming the best version of yourself, negative emotions get diluted. Frustration, anger, disappointment, guilt, regret, anxiety, irritability, insecurity start to fade away and are replaced with more joy, gratitude, pride, confidence and love. It is time for you to head more in this direction.

By integrating these exercises into your daily life, you'll quickly develop a Stoic mindset—calm, rational and resilient in the face of life's uncertainties. It's amazing how quickly it becomes habit if you are disciplined from the outset.

You will learn more about Stoicism as you turn the pages and we will examine living like a Stoic in Chapter 13. For now, let's focus on why you need not only learn about Stoicism (or any other philosophy), but continue to keep the knowledge flowing and create a life of continuous learning. To foster personal growth, adaptability and resilience in an ever-changing world. To cultivate a growth mindset, allowing you to embrace challenges and seize opportunities, expand your horizon, promote self-awareness and nurture your curiosity.

CHAPTER 3

# WHY YOU NEED TO READ, LEARN AND KEEP THE KNOWLEDGE FLOWING

*"Wisdom is not a product of schooling but of the lifelong attempt to acquire it."*
— Albert Einstein

From 2004 until 2009, I plugged away at a Master of Business degree. I played first-grade rugby during this time and I would go straight from work to training three nights a week. Saturday, game day, was spent at the oval supporting the lower grades until my feature game at 3:15 pm. Post-match functions would lead into an all-night binge session, and Sunday was a write-off. Bruised and battered, often concussed, and nursing a night drenched in booze, it was a wasted day with me blended into the sofa, feeling sorry for myself.

There was so much reading material in my study obligations, thick, heavy textbooks and course notes, that I spent every weekday pre-dawn reading enough to get a pass at the close of each semester. After five years of slogging out the degree, I stupidly branded myself as someone who didn't like to read books. I didn't plan to pick up another. It wasn't until 2022 that I read my next book, gifted by my sister, to help manage my emotional trauma. The book was *Letting*

*Go: The Pathway of Surrender* by David Hawkins. I will address this book in Chapter 9.

I'm not one to dwell on the past, because it can't be altered, but I regret missing out on so much knowledge in the 13 years I disconnected from literature. Regret, when harnessed correctly, can be a powerful catalyst for transformation. Instead of dwelling guiltily on past mistakes, regret can serve as a reminder of what needs to change and fuel the determination to do better. It sharpens self-awareness, helping to refine choices and break negative patterns. When used constructively, regret pushes you to take action, ensuring that past missteps become stepping stones rather than stumbling blocks. In this way, regret becomes a force that propels you forward towards growth and success, not a weight that holds you back.

Insatiable curiosity lies at the heart of the human experience—a relentless desire to explore, discover and understand. Think back to childhood, when every day was an adventure and each moment promised something new. That same spirit of curiosity is not a relic of our youth, but a beacon lighting the way to happiness.

When we read or listen to audiobooks and embrace a mindset of continual learning, we rekindle our curiosity. We approach each day with wonder, eager to absorb the lessons of literature and life. Whether we are delving into a new skill, immersing ourselves in a different culture, or simply pondering life's mysteries, each opportunity to learn something new becomes a source of joy.

As we journey alongside authors' personal experiences, from their diverse backgrounds and perspectives, we are granted a window into their innermost thoughts, feelings and struggles. Through this process, we develop a deeper understanding of the human condition, learning to see the world through the eyes of others. We learn to appreciate the complexities of each individual's journey and, in doing so, we foster a sense of connection and belonging that transcends the boundaries of race, religion and culture.

Through the pages of books, we gain access to the accumulated wisdom of generations past, tapping into the insights of philosophers, scholars and visionaries who have grappled with the fundamental questions of existence. In a world marked by uncertainty and change, this pursuit of wisdom offers us a compass by which to navigate the complexities of life. Whether we seek guidance on matters of love and relationships, wisdom in the face of adversity, or clarity in times of confusion, the pages of a book stand ready to offer us counsel and companionship on our journey.

In an age of screens, devices, social media and constant distraction, reading offers us a rare opportunity to cultivate mindfulness and presence. When we lose ourselves in a book, our minds are fully engaged in the present moment, free from the incessant chatter of worries and obligations. In this state of focused attention, we experience a profound sense of peace and clarity as the outside world's noise fades into the background.

Reading can also become a form of meditation as we immerse ourselves in the rhythm of words and sentences, allowing our thoughts to flow freely and our imaginations to soar. In these moments of quiet contemplation, we find respite from the frenetic pace of modern life and reconnect with the deeper currents of our inner selves.

****

Please go down all the rabbit holes that this book may present and continue your thirst for more information, knowledge and wisdom to progress in building your system for happiness. I don't have many answers, but I have advice that can motivate you to keep searching, asking questions and acquiring wisdom—positive wisdom you can share with the world and make it a better place. Each step in this modern world forces us to learn so we don't trip. Embrace this opportunity and run towards educating your mind. Those who embrace lifelong learning are not merely survivors; they are thrivers. Learning becomes a response to change and a catalyst for growth and resilience.

Seneca says, "As long as you live, keep learning how to live." When we commit ourselves to continuous learning, we cultivate a growth mindset—a belief in our capacity to adapt, evolve and overcome challenges. Each new piece of knowledge, every skill mastered, becomes a building block in the fortress of our resilience. In the face of adversity, this resilience becomes our shield, allowing us to weather life's storms with grace and fortitude.

When we engage in learning that aligns with our passions and values, we tap into a wellspring of purpose that nourishes our souls. Whether pursuing a lifelong dream, making a difference in our communities, or simply striving to be the best version of ourselves, each step we take on the learning journey brings us closer to fulfilling our purpose.

Through reading and my reignited desire to learn, I have sat with Victor Frankl, an Austrian psychiatrist and Holocaust survivor, while he found meaning in a patient's life through logotherapy. I have stood under an ancient Greek stoa (covered walkway) with Zeno of Citium as he orated that universal reason was the greatest good in life and living in accordance with reason was the purpose of human life. I have hovered over Nero, the fifth emperor of Rome, notorious for his cruelty and debauchery, while Seneca, his adviser, tutored his wayward mind. I have gardened in Okinawa with centenarians and listened to why their community has a life expectancy much higher than the global average.

After the last chapter of this book, pick up another, then another. Turn the radio off in the car and play another podcast about forming better habits. Remove the screen from the bedroom and go to sleep listening to Alan Watts unravel the mysteries of life. Embark on a journey of discovery and learning that transcends the mere act of flipping pages and immerse yourself in the world created by the author. Explore new perspectives, cultures, concepts and emotions by encountering unfamiliar landscapes, both physical and metaphorical, and broaden your understanding of the world.

Seek material that stimulates reflection on your experiences, beliefs and values in light of what you absorb in each book. This reflection undoubtedly leads to personal growth and self-awareness. The opportunity for learning is infinite. Reading is inherently educational, whether it's acquiring new information, gaining insights into human nature, or expanding one's vocabulary.

Challenge your preconceived notions and beliefs and allow yourself to be pushed out of your comfort zone. This challenge is essential for intellectual growth and critical thinking. Let reading and learning do their magic, leading to your transformation. By accumulating knowledge, empathy and understanding, you will emerge from each new book or podcast changed— with a shift in perspective, a new-found passion, or a deeper appreciation for the world around you.

Please don't make the mistake that I made and not find time to read. You're reading this now, so you are already in positive momentum. The journey never ends when the book is closed. Carry your insights and experiences gained from each book into your daily life. Let it influence decisions, interactions and perceptions long after you have read it. So, let's embark on this journey together, with open minds and hearts, for the joy of learning knows no bounds, and the adventure of discovery awaits us at every turn.

If you're a reader, well done. Keep the pages turning.

If you are not a reader, as I was, and this is a one-off book, read three more books over the next 12 months. That's only one book a quarter, or four for the year. Make it a goal and hold yourself to it. When you make your bed in the morning, make it a habit to leave your book on the pillow so you can't get into the bed without making physical contact with it. If you are tired or not up for reading, set a target of reading just one page; chances are you will read a few more.

Pairing my reading with my winding down for bed has been an ingredient in my improved sleep. Make it a habit to reduce whatever distractions you can, to help you focus. I also enjoy reading multiple books at once, covering various genres. Chipping away at all of them. Work on making reading a pleasure, not a chore.

Listen to podcasts in the car. They are highly accessible and convenient, allowing you to enjoy content on demand anytime, anywhere. Podcasts are excellent tools for continuous learning and self-improvement. When you are driving and you hear a piece of content you don't want to forget, say, "Hey, Siri, make a note", and then detail the information so you can return to your notes to create and curate what you have learnt.

## REMEMBER THIS

It is my belief, through lived experience and improving my life, that you need to be growth oriented. Stay curious and open-minded, always embracing opportunities to learn and grow. Cultivating a continuous learning mindset allows you to gain new knowledge and insights, broadening your perspective and enriching your understanding of the world. This openness to new experiences and ideas strengthens your resolve and equips you with the adaptability to navigate and thrive in an ever-changing environment. By constantly seeking out fresh experiences and remaining receptive to diverse viewpoints, you can enhance your ability to respond to challenges with resilience and creativity, ultimately fostering personal and professional growth.

CHAPTER 4

# DISCIPLINE, DISCIPLINE, DISCIPLINE

*"If you can change your mind, you can change your life."*
— William James

I love it when you're crafting your path towards being healthy, emotionally balanced and disciplined, and a professional validates your actions with experience and evidence-based thought leadership.

I was deep into another subject area, unrelated to discipline, when I stumbled across a YouTube video of Dr James Rouse talking about Phil Stutz's three disciplines: structural, expansive and reactive. Some content grabs you straight away, while other content blows by. This concept of the three disciplines resonated with me because it validated my thoughts and connected many of my wellness intentions and strategies.

Phil Stutz, a renowned psychiatrist and co-author of *The Tools* with Barry Michels, has developed a framework to help people overcome personal obstacles and achieve personal growth. Central to his philosophy are the three disciplines: structural discipline, expansive discipline, and reactive discipline. These disciplines serve as guiding principles for self-mastery and resilience in facing life's challenges. Understanding and applying them can lead to a more fulfilling and purpose-driven life. I had been focused on all these disciplines in many ways, but it's excellent to put additional context around it.

This chapter focuses heavily on structural discipline, the foundation of personal and professional success. It refers to the ability to create and maintain a structured routine that supports stability and progress. Stutz emphasises that a strong structure provides predictability, reduces anxiety and helps us focus on our goals. Discipline involves setting clear priorities, managing time effectively, and cultivating habits that align with our long-term aspirations. For me, this is about establishing a morning routine that includes exercise, mindfulness and setting goals. You develop resilience against distractions and external pressures by consistently following a structure. Ultimately, structural discipline fosters self-discipline and helps us stay grounded in our commitments. I will get more into this in a sec.

Expansive discipline involves continuously pushing beyond comfort zones and seeking personal growth. Combined with expanding your knowledge, as I've detailed in Chapter 3, it requires us to challenge ourselves, embrace uncertainty, and develop a mindset of curiosity and exploration.

This is why I have come up with "50by50"; 50 challenges to attempt by the age of 51. I'm not trying to influence anyone reading this to do the same. I want you to set some big goals, go after them, and grow through the process, but there's no expectation for the number of goals. For me, setting such a high number is exclusive to me.

According to Stutz, growth happens when we take proactive steps towards learning new skills, building relationships and facing our fears. A practical example of expansive discipline is a professional taking on new challenges at work, even when they are unprepared. By stepping outside their comfort zone, they expand their capabilities and confidence. This discipline encourages people to view setbacks as learning experiences rather than failures, leading to a more dynamic and adaptive approach to life.

Reactive discipline focuses on how we respond to adversity and setbacks. Life is unpredictable and challenges are inevitable; what matters most is how we react to difficulties. This is how I landed on Stoicism and aligned with this philosophy so naturally. It's also why I dedicated Chapter 13 to "letting go", which isn't in opposition to Stoicism but is a perfectly weighted balance to manage the thoughts in your life that need to be surrendered.

Later in the book I will cover the balance between dedicated effort and letting go of attachment to outcomes by engaging fully in our pursuits with passion and discipline while at the same time accepting that we cannot control every result. Stutz teaches us that we must cultivate resilience by positively and proactively responding to obstacles. Practising reactive discipline involves recognising negative emotions, reframing problems as opportunities, and taking constructive action despite discomfort. For example, when facing rejection or failure, a person with strong reactive discipline might focus on what they can learn from the experience, rather than dwelling on their disappointment. This mindset allows you to recover quickly and continue pursuing your goals without being paralysed by self-doubt or fear. This aligns with Stoicism because it embodies the philosophy's emphasis on controlling one's perception, managing emotions and taking purposeful action.

As you know, Stoics believe that external events are beyond our control, but our reactions to them are within our power. We practice the Stoic virtues of wisdom and courage by recognising negative emotions without being ruled by them, reframing obstacles as opportunities for growth, and responding rationally. Like the Stoic principle of *amor fati*—embracing fate and using adversity for self-improvement—reactive discipline enables you to remain steadfast in your pursuits despite setbacks, embodying the Stoic ideal of inner tranquillity amid life's challenges.

Phil Stutz's three disciplines—structural, expansive and reactive—offer a comprehensive approach to self-development and resilience. Before stumbling upon Stutz's theory, I had integrated these principles into my daily life, achieving excellent results over the last few years and cultivating a stronger sense of purpose, adaptability and inner strength. Stutz has emphasised that these disciplines are not just theoretical concepts. They are practical tools that, when consistently applied, can lead to a more fulfilling life. I will focus more on structural discipline, as it lays the groundwork for stability and focus. However, expansive and reactive aspects are well covered throughout this book through my own practical lens.

In specific periods of my life I have had an abundance of discipline, while at other times I have had almost none.

I had military-style discipline in my attention to sporting goals, particularly during my senior year of high school and my professional years in rugby. I was small in physical stature for a rugby player, but being a lightweight never affected me from a defensive perspective. In the late 1990s, I played 27 consecutive games without missing a tackle, and in most of those games, my team lost. As an outside back, I needed to make as many tackles as possible, as the team's defensive line wasn't secure enough to win. In 2000, I played three Super Rugby games for the Waratahs. In those three games, I made more tackles that season than any other Super Rugby winger (my position) and many wingers in the competition played more than 10 games. Defence is five per cent size, 10 per cent technique, and 85 per cent willpower.

However, being small from an attacking perspective, I lacked the physical capability to steamroll over the top of the opposition if I was running in a straight line. To limit injuries, it was in my best interest to dance around would-be tacklers, especially as the game drew closer to the full-time whistle and the opposition's fatigue became an opportunity to break through the defensive line. I needed to stand out to be selected for representative teams. To stand out, I needed to make try-saving tackles and score tries. I needed to be the fittest player in each game I played.

I was disciplined about my fitness during the season and even more disciplined about self-management in the off-season. I did everything I was asked—and more. I was the fittest player on every team I played for, as well as in the broader Australian rugby competition.

This was supported by the highest beep test recorded in my time. The beep test is a reliable, standardised cardiovascular endurance test. The test requires running back and forth between two points 20 metres apart. You must maintain a running speed determined by a pre-set audio tone that sounds like a "beep" throughout the test duration. The required running speed or pace increases as the test progresses. You run to the opposing 20-metre endpoint and arrive when the tone sounds again. Then, you need to return to your starting point again for the following beep. The speed you need to maintain remains constant throughout each "level", which lasts approximately one minute. At the end of each level, a triple beep will indicate that a new level is commencing. At the start of a new level, the required running speed increases. You run until you can't keep up with the beep, and your score is recorded at the level you drop out.

I scored 15-10 in a beep test, the highest score recorded in Australian rugby. Every club, state and international team used the test to benchmark their players. Being disciplined and exceptionally fit helped me get selected for representative teams and laid the foundation for some of my most vivid sporting and life memories. One memory was getting off to a shaky first half in the mud, then scoring three tries in the second half of my first-grade debut at age 18. Another notable achievement was scoring the winning try against Samoa in a global tournament, which secured the Australian Sevens team's spot in the final against New Zealand, a match we subsequently won at a fully packed stadium in Paris. In the 1998 Australian under-20 team, we needed to secure four tries in the final against Argentina to win the World Championship in Cape Town. I crossed the line not long before the game's conclusion, far from where I was expected to be positioned on the field, securing the points needed to seal the game and win the championship. Highlights like this wouldn't exist without the self-discipline that was the building block that incrementally transported me to that time and place through consistent, unwavering effort. You might think, Well, I'm not an athlete, so I don't need to be that disciplined. These were simply the fruits of my goals at the time and the discipline required to achieve them.

It's all relative to what you want to achieve. Through my experience and evaluation, I need to return to a professional athlete-type discipline to elevate my happiness and allow me to flourish. The reward is much greater than scoring tries and winning games. My reward is increased happiness, and while I have detailed my definition of happiness in Chapter 1, it aligns with Aristotle's belief that happiness is the highest good and the ultimate goal of human existence.

\*\*\*\*

What is a period of your life when you were most disciplined? Was it your childhood, the structured school years? Teenage years with exam preparation? College or university, competitive courses, when studying for demanding degrees or professional certifications? Was it your first job that helped you build your work ethic and establish credibility? Or was it with competitive sports or fitness goals, such as training for competitions or major fitness milestones? When forming a routine, was it carrying a baby or parenthood, especially with young kids? Was it a religious or spiritual commitment when managing schedules, routines and responsibilities during fasting, pilgrimage or dedicated spiritual practices? Was it a medical or health recovery, post-surgery or managing chronic illness when following strict health protocols? Something else? Discipline often peaks during high-stakes situations, personal growth or when external structure is in place. Take a moment to revisit that period of immense mental discipline. It's in you.

I have also been at the other end of the discipline paradigm, powerless against alcohol and recreational drugs that continued to steal my happiness from the proceeding days. This widely accepted abuse was the most significant ingredient in dropping my daily mood to subpar standards. I barely showed even occasional piecemeal discipline in abating my binge drinking for more than 20 years before I finally made significant changes. I learnt that a lack of discipline in one area of life often creates a domino effect, influencing other aspects in ways we may not immediately recognise. Discipline is a skill that strengthens with use. When we allow ourselves to slack off in one area—whether it's excessive drinking without control, poor health, financial struggles or strained relationships—it becomes easier to justify a lack of discipline elsewhere. Even small things, such as skipping workouts, can lead to unhealthy eating habits, which in turn affect energy levels and productivity at work. Over time, lower standards become the norm. When inconsistency is tolerated in one aspect of life, it gradually seeps into others.

Beyond this, a lack of discipline erodes self-trust. Each time we break a commitment to ourselves, we reinforce the belief that our word doesn't matter, whether that's to ourselves or to others. This gradual loss of self-respect can make it even harder to stay motivated in other areas. The stress resulting from unfinished tasks, financial strain or poor health choices can drain us emotionally and mentally, reducing the energy we need to maintain discipline. Momentum plays a decisive role in both discipline and laziness. Just as staying committed in one area can have a positive influence on others, failing to maintain discipline can lead to a downward spiral. A messy room can lead to a cluttered mind, which in turn can result in procrastination at work, missed opportunities, and an overall feeling of being stuck.

There were stretches of my life where I found myself wholly trapped in self-destructive cycles. Vices became my crutch. Whether it was unhealthy habits, mindless distractions or toxic routines, they consumed me. My diet deteriorated to the point where I barely paid attention to what I was putting into my body. My fitness levels plummeted; workouts became a distant memory, and even basic movement felt like a chore. Any drive or ambition I once had seemed to dissolve, leaving me running on empty, operating at a fraction of my true potential. It was more than just a slump—it was a suffocating state of existence. The deeper I sank, the harder it became to see a way out. Stress, anxiety and depression took turns weighing me down, amplifying feelings of self-doubt and worthlessness. Every day felt like a losing battle, as if I were stuck in quicksand, sinking inch by inch, with no rope to pull myself free. The harder I struggled, the more I felt trapped, reinforcing the belief that this was the way things were meant to be.

It's a dark place to be—one that warps your sense of self and convinces you that change is impossible. However, the truth is that even in those moments, there is still a way forward. It may not be apparent or straightforward, but it's there, waiting to be found.

The good news is that rebuilding discipline doesn't require an overnight transformation. Small, intentional actions—such as making your bed, changing what you eat for breakfast, sticking to a morning routine or setting a daily goal—can create positive momentum that gradually carries over into other areas of life. Discipline in multiple small areas collectively has a considerable impact because small, consistent actions accumulate over time, leading to significant transformations. Actual progress is built on the foundation of minor, disciplined habits practised daily.

For instance, maintaining discipline in areas such as waking up early, organising your workspace, exercising daily, managing time effectively and practising gratitude might seem insignificant on their own. But combined, they create a structured, efficient and productive lifestyle. Similarly, consistently meeting deadlines, improving communication, staying organised and refining your skills in small increments in professional settings contribute to long-term success and career growth. In financial management, simple habits such as tracking expenses, saving a small percentage of your income and avoiding unnecessary purchases can lead to financial stability over time.

The cumulative effect of these disciplined efforts is greater efficiency, enhanced wellbeing and increased opportunities. Just as a drop of water repeatedly hitting a rock eventually shapes it, disciplined micro-actions shape a person's success, resilience and overall quality of life. Mastering small commitments strengthens discipline, and soon order replaces chaos, self-trust grows, and life begins to flow more smoothly.

Willpower, much like muscle, grows stronger with consistent use and practice. Just as lifting weights helps build physical strength, challenging your self-control can gradually build mental resilience. You train your willpower each time you push through discomfort or resist a short-term temptation for a long-term benefit. As your willpower strengthens, you'll find taking on more significant challenges easier, just as an athlete increases their training intensity over time. Building your willpower is about more than resisting temptations. It's about shaping your mindset to prioritise lasting fulfilment over immediate gratification. With repeated practice and small, intentional steps, you can turn your willpower into a robust and reliable ally for reaching your goals.

Some of your goals need to be significant. While many small habit changes significantly impact your life, I made some big changes to move the needle aggressively. I encourage you to do the same. Making massive changes can be challenging. If it were easy, we would all have reached Buddhist monk-style enlightenment already. Unwavering self-discipline is complex and requires a combination of mental, emotional and behavioural qualities. Many ingredients are needed to become more disciplined, and the biggest of all is defining your goals and the reasons behind them. Discipline is present when you are motivated by goals. When you have a clear sense of purpose, it becomes easier to stay disciplined because you know what you're working towards.

****

Write down your wellness goals and consider adopting a couple of mine as your own. Set a minimum time of 12 months for the goals so they become a new way of life for you.

Consider:
1. Stop drinking alcohol.
2. Cut out sugar and starch.
3. Wake up an hour earlier.
4. Journal daily.
5. Read three more books after this one.
6. Sign up for one physical event and train for it.
7. Learn a new sport or practical activity.
8. Stay off your phone for the first hour, social media for the first three hours of your waking day, and an hour before sleep.

9. Practice mindfulness more than three times a week.
10. Become a student of Stoic philosophy.
11. Move your body every weekday.

You can only adopt these goals if you genuinely think you can attain them. If you have a list of your own goals mixed with some of mine, it's a lot. Are you capable? I will ask again … are you capable?

****

As you examine your documented goals, think about each one while recognising your strengths and weaknesses, and the triggers that might lead you astray. Self-awareness allows you to anticipate challenges and develop strategies to overcome them. Make a firm decision to pursue your goals and stick to them, even when faced with obstacles or temptations. Commitment requires dedication and perseverance. Establish consistent routines and habits that support your goals. Consistency builds momentum and reinforces self-discipline over time. Accept that setbacks are a natural part of the journey and view them as opportunities for growth rather than reasons to give up. Develop resilience to bounce back from failures and setbacks more robustly than before. Remember why you are going after these goals. You want to feel good. You want to feel amazing. You want to be happy—or happier than you are now. You want to flourish.

Self-discipline helps you to realise your full potential, making consistent effort, attaining goals, and resilience in the face of adversity easier. Embodying discipline in your actions and decisions unlocks the keys to self-mastery and the path to enduring success and fulfilment. You need a great deal of discipline to wake up early, read and learn more, change daily habits, reduce alcohol consumption to zero, eat healthily, sleep better, and develop and focus on your purpose in life. Self-discipline fosters the ability to stay focused in the face of distractions, safeguarding you from deviating from your chosen path.

In an age characterised by constant stimulation and competing demands for our attention, the capacity to maintain focus is invaluable. We can optimise productivity and effectiveness by cultivating the discipline to prioritise tasks and allocate resources judiciously. Self-discipline lays the foundation for developing constructive habits that underpin long-term success. By consistently engaging in behaviours that promote growth and progress, we ingrain positive routines that propel us towards our desired outcomes. Whether it's dedicating time to learning, maintaining a healthy lifestyle, or nurturing relationships, self-discipline empowers us to cultivate habits that help our personal and professional development.

Someone wise once said, "Discipline will take you places motivation can't." Some people reading this are thinking this whole discipline initiative sounds scary and hard. Being extremely disciplined can sound frightening and too challenging to accomplish, because it often implies rigid control, sacrifice, and an intense level of commitment that many find overwhelming. Discipline is usually associated with strict routines and restrictions, leading people to worry that they'll lose their spontaneity, creativity or ability to enjoy life freely.

Holding yourself to a high standard may create pressure and fear of failure, making some feel like a mistake could ruin their progress. As discussed, discipline demands consistency, which can feel exhausting and perhaps even unsustainable over time.

Another concern for you may be a fear of missing out. Being disciplined often requires saying no to temptations, whether it's indulging in unhealthy food, attending social outings, having beers or cocktails with friends, or choosing to work instead of relaxing. This can make you feel like you're missing out on enjoyable experiences. Past failures can also contribute to self-doubt, making it seem impossible to maintain discipline in the long term. Many, like the old me, adopt an all-or-nothing mindset, believing they've failed if they can't be perfectly disciplined at all times. This black-and-white thinking makes the goal seem unreachable.

You may also feel that extreme discipline can be isolating. If others around you don't share the same mindset, it might create social challenges and a sense of loneliness. But the truth is that balance is key. While extreme discipline may seem intimidating, developing sustainable habits rather than striving for perfection is a more practical approach. Discipline doesn't have to mean deprivation—it simply means making intentional choices that align with your goals, big or small.

One of the most significant rewards of discipline that I've experienced firsthand is that strictness and routine become a way of life. What was hard is now easy. Discipline is challenging at first because it requires breaking away from comfort, bad habits, and the pursuit of instant gratification. The initial phase feels uncomfortable and painful because the mind and body resist change.

But as you push through the early struggles, discipline feels less like a burden and more like a habit. The brain adapts, routines become second nature, and the rewards of discipline—such as increased productivity, better health, personal growth and an elevated base happiness—start to reinforce the behaviour. Over time, what once felt difficult becomes automatic, even enjoyable. At this point, discipline transforms into a way of life. You no longer have to force yourself to stay consistent, because it becomes an integral part of your identity. Instead of relying on fleeting motivation, you develop a strong foundation of habits that effortlessly guide your actions.

While what was hard becomes easy. You always need discipline as you continue to add new goals and form new habits, like working hard every day, even when you don't feel like it. Discipline needs to be an integral part of who you are. It is not about restriction or self-denial, but rather about achieving freedom, excellence and purpose through self-control, encompassing physical, mental and moral dimensions.

\*\*\*\*

Stoicism and discipline are deeply connected. Stoicism emphasises self-control, resilience and rational decision-making—key elements of discipline. Stoicism teaches people to master their emotions, urging them not to be controlled by anger, fear or desire. Discipline, in turn, requires the ability to act rationally despite emotional impulses. A core Stoic principle focuses on what is within our control, which is essential to discipline as it helps avoid distractions and maintain a commitment to goals. Stoicism also encourages endurance through hardship, promoting the idea that challenges should be faced with a steady mind. Discipline mirrors this by pushing us to persist even when our motivation fades. The philosophy also values daily habits, self-reflection and constant self-improvement, which align with disciplined routines.

Stoicism emphasises delayed gratification, favouring wisdom and long-term thinking over short-term pleasure. This self-restraint is a fundamental aspect of discipline, ensuring that we stay on the right path despite temptations. In essence, Stoicism provides the mindset while discipline is the action that brings it to life.

\*\*\*\*

I like Ryan Holiday's exploration of discipline as a foundational pillar of success and moral excellence in his book *Discipline is Destiny*. He uses Stoic philosophy, historical examples and personal insights to demonstrate that discipline is not merely about restriction or self-denial, but rather about achieving freedom, excellence and purpose through self-control. His definition of discipline is broad yet deeply practical, taking in physical, mental and moral dimensions.

At the heart of Holiday's definition is the idea of self-mastery. He argues that discipline is about controlling one's impulses, emotions and actions to align them with a greater goal. He emphasises that true discipline is not about punishment or suffering, but about making intentional choices that lead to a better life. He cites historical figures like Marcus Aurelius, George Washington and Lou Gehrig as examples of people who embodied this principle through their steadfast commitment to self-control.

Holiday also defines discipline as the ability to show up consistently, even when it is difficult. He discusses how many of history's most outstanding leaders and thinkers succeeded not because of talent alone, but because they disciplined themselves to work hard every day. In this sense, discipline is about the long game—doing what needs to be done, whether or not one feels like it.

Beyond personal ambition, Holiday frames discipline as a moral duty. He argues that self-discipline is not just about achieving success, but is also about doing what is right even when no one is watching. He contrasts this with indulgence and impulsivity, which often have negative consequences. He suggests that a disciplined person lives by principles rather than by fleeting desires, reinforcing the Stoic belief that virtue is the highest good.

One of Holiday's most compelling arguments is that discipline ultimately leads to freedom. While it may seem paradoxical, he explains that those who lack discipline become slaves to their emotions, cravings and distractions. By contrast, those who master themselves gain control over their lives and decisions. This concept aligns with the Stoic idea that true freedom comes from self-restraint rather than indulgence. Holiday defines discipline as the key to a meaningful and fulfilling life. It is not about harshness or deprivation, but about self-mastery, consistency, moral integrity and true freedom. By practising discipline, people can achieve excellence in their personal and professional lives while contributing positively to the world. Discipline is not a means to an end, but a way of living.

## REMEMBER THIS

I can't find the source of this quotation, but this definition hits home for me: "Discipline is the strongest form of self-love. It's ignoring something you want right now for something better later on. Discipline reveals the commitment you have to your dreams. Especially on days you don't want to. The future you is depending on the current you to keep the promises you made to yourself yesterday."

CHAPTER 5

# HABITS, CHANGE THEM

*"We are what we repeatedly do.
Excellence, then, is not an act, but a habit."*
— Aristotle

I used the word "habit" 16 times in the last chapter, a strong indicator that a chapter on habits should follow after a chapter on discipline, right?

For years, I found myself drawn to the familiar weight of my smartphone. That black 15 x 7 cm device became an integral part of my daily routine, a constant companion in a world where screens glow brighter than stars and notifications sing their siren songs. Each day seemed to blur into the next, with my phone always within arm's reach. From the moment I woke until I finally succumbed to sleep, my hand instinctively reached for that glowing screen. In the quiet moments before the day truly begins, I found myself lost in a sea of emails, messages, news updates and the drug of social media. Time slipped through my fingers unnoticed, leaving behind a residue of anxiety and distraction. Throughout the day, my phone remained my constant companion, a shield against boredom and a conduit for connection, but a shift from being present in the moment. Before sleep, my phone would illuminate my face with blue light, the part of the light spectrum most active in our sleep cycle, actively suppressing the production of melatonin and keeping my brain active when it should be winding down.

I have homed in on my phone use because it was the first habit I focused on when revolutionising my life. It's also a harmful habit that I know I share with so many people. Meaninglessly checking my phone made me feel anxious. I craved constant stimulation, felt restless or uncomfortable without the distraction and engagement. I had no social comparison issues, but I was interested in following people's embellished and curated online personas. My excessive phone use distracted me from important tasks or responsibilities, leading to anxiety about falling behind or not meeting deadlines.

While it is not a feeling I have ever experienced, several people close to me suffer from FOMO (fear of missing out) as they worry about being left out or disconnected from their social circle. The phone would play a significant role in exacerbating this emotion, I'm sure.

My phone hasn't been my only vice. I have procrastinated at different times, putting off tasks until the last minute, or indefinitely. For decades, I made excessive alcohol consumption a regular part of life, drinking booze to the point of inebriation every week and always lighting up a smoke or puffing on a vape as soon as I was drunk. Up until 2023, I was a junk food binger, regularly consuming large quantities of unhealthy or processed foods in just a handful of minutes. I've occasionally fallen into poor time management, frequently running late or failing to complete tasks on time. I've been a binge streamer, watching television shows or movies for extended periods without breaks. I've been stuck in periods of little or no exercise, not engaging in regular physical activity for weeks or months.

****

Bad habits often lead to negative consequences in various aspects of life, such as health, relationships, work and personal fulfilment. These consequences can cause stress, guilt and dissatisfaction. The negative emotions can erode self-esteem and overall wellbeing. Bad habits can interfere with our ability to achieve our goals and fulfil our potential. When we repeatedly engage in behaviours that sabotage our progress, it can lead to frustration and dissatisfaction with ourselves and our lives.

Many bad habits, such as smoking, excessive drinking, poor diet and lack of exercise, have a direct negative impact on physical and mental health. Poor health can significantly reduce quality of life. Bad habits often consume time and energy that could be better spent on productive or fulfilling activities. Engaging in activities that provide little or no benefit can leave us feeling unfulfilled and dissatisfied. Some bad habits, such as substance abuse or compulsive behaviours, can lead to addiction. Addiction can trap us in a cycle of craving, consumption and temporary relief, followed by guilt, shame, and worsening consequences. This cycle can perpetuate unhappiness, making it difficult to break free from the habit.

In the labyrinth of human behaviour, habits serve as the guiding threads that lead us through our daily lives. They are the invisible hands that shape our actions, thoughts and, ultimately, our destinies. From the mundane rituals of brushing teeth to the complex routines of professional athletes, habits define the contours of our existence. Yet their significance extends beyond routine; they profoundly influence our health, productivity and happiness.

Before embarking on the journey of habit transformation, it's essential to understand its essence. At their core, habits are ingrained patterns of behaviour acquired through repetition. They operate within the intricate circuitry of our brains, forming neural pathways that streamline our actions. Whether it's the habit of procrastination or the discipline of exercise, these behavioural loops shape our identities and mould our realities.

Humans are creatures of habit, often finding comfort in the familiar rhythms of our daily lives. However, this penchant for routine can sometimes lead to stagnation and complacency. When we remain shackled to destructive habits, we relinquish control over our lives, allowing inertia to dictate our destinies. The consequences of inertia are profound, whether it's a sedentary lifestyle that undermines our health or negative thought patterns that erode our mental wellbeing.

The pivotal question then arises: why change our habits? The answer lies in the boundless potential that lies dormant within each of us. By undoing the shackles of old habits and embracing new ones, we unlock the gates to personal growth and self-actualisation. Whether we are pursuing physical fitness, cultivating mindfulness, or developing professional skills, transforming habits is the cornerstone of progress.

One of the most remarkable features of the human brain is its capacity for neuroplasticity—the ability to rewire its neural networks in response to experience. This forms the bedrock of habit transformation, enabling us to carve new behaviour pathways through deliberate practice and repetition. By harnessing the power of neuroplasticity, we can reprogram our minds, transcending the limitations of our past selves and forging new trajectories for the future.

\*\*\*\*

Looking through my journal, I committed to making significant habit changes at the beginning of 2023. These are the primary habits I focused on for that year, and I attribute them to my increased happiness.

The habits I dropped:
- Reduced social media consumption by 90 per cent
- Reading or watching zero news during the weekdays—this organically became zero news consumption
- No alcohol for 365 days. This is now 1,000 days and counting
- Reduced sugar and starch consumption by over 90 per cent

These are the habits I picked up:
- Falling in love with my routine!
- Reading and learning daily
- Journalling
- I am working through my 50by50 goals, which contain tasks associated with movement, balance, mindfulness, strength, speed, and even a sprinkle of stupidity
- Stretching and then jumping in the ocean every weekday morning
- More than two Pilates classes a week
- Regular cold swims or plunges
- Eating a diet focused on reducing inflammation
- Surrendering to many emotional feelings and learning to let go of emotions

Thanks to neuroplasticity, I have rewired my brain so these things are now part of my daily routine. I have subsequently stacked multiple additional healthy habits on top, many small, but collectively large. Since making these changes, I've read several books on habits to broaden my knowledge. Still, I had not read any material on the subject at the start of my habit transformation effort, which was meaningful to me as the demand for change came from within. So why and how did I make these dramatic changes?

The spark for me was simply the vision I had for myself 30 years from now. Life moves so fast, and I needed to change the trajectory to ensure a healthy and happy 90-year-old me in 2068. This was the spark that ignited my discipline for change.

At 40, I began to notice dramatic changes in the physical appearance of my circle of friends. It felt like the halfway point, where you need to choose a direction before life beats you down. Around the same time as noticing people age dramatically, Louise passed away, and I put all the energy I had into looking after Noah and Evie. A three-year old and a five-year-old can't function and survive without parental support. I wanted the transition of losing a parent to be as non-disruptive as humanly possible for my kids. For not a single second did I want my wife's babies to feel like I was handing their care to anyone else, so I committed to supporting them in every way that Lou and I would have done combined. Any single parent knows that with a toddler or preschooler, if you need milk or bread or something from the chemist, it's a family trip, no matter the time. With two connected physical and emotional dependents in all that you do, time is like water in a sieve.

In the year of Lou's death, Noah was starting primary school and Evie was still at daycare three times a week, so this meant multiple car trips and time commitments for school, sport and their little social engagements. Pouring all my energy and emotions into my children's love cup and not leaving any for my own was a significant contributor to my breakdown. I needed more time to devote to my healing process, which included professional therapy. But where the fuck was I going to find more time?

Going from two incomes to one and instantly becoming a full-time single parent was an adjustment for me. For the first five years after Louise died, I spent more money annually than I earned, so I had to find not just more time for myself for a better self-love balance, but also more time to work and increase my income before going negative on our savings before Noah and Evie started high school with high tuition fees.

With my back against the wall, I began searching for a way to source time. After experimenting with self-made spreadsheets, I needed to squeeze every minute wherever possible.

- I found 35,000 Netflix minutes a year that I could use
- I found 10,950 minutes by reducing my daily news consumption by 30 minutes, to zero
- I found 10,000 minutes a year by deleting the Facebook app from my phone and reducing my Instagram use by more than 50%
- I found over 31,200 minutes a year by not drinking, along with about 25,000 minutes of useless hangover time, where I would achieve almost nothing

With this alone, I found more than 11 weeks a year to do things that, near the end of my life, I would wish I had spent more time on.

1 day = 1,440 minutes

$$\frac{112{,}150}{1{,}440} \approx 77.84 \text{ days}$$

**112,150 minutes is approximately 77.84 days**, or about **77 days and 20 hours.**

No one has ever got to the end of their life and said:
- "I wish I'd watched more news so I was more informed."
- "I wish I'd binged more Netflix."
- "I wish I'd drunk more wine."
- "I wish I'd browsed more social media."
- "I wish I'd taken more recreational drugs."
- "I wish I'd slept in more when I was young and healthy."

- "I wish I'd moved less."
- "I wish I'd spent less time with my children."
- "I wish I'd worked more and not followed my dream."
- "I wish I hadn't focused on my health so much."
- "I wish I didn't give back and help others or contribute to the community."
- "I wish I'd ignored my intuition and not listened to my gut feelings and instincts."

> *"Your habits will determine your future."*
> — Jack Canfield

\*\*\*\*

Start replacing bad habits with good ones today. Take control of your narrative, and start writing a better story for yourself now.

- Delete your news apps from your phone. Remove suggested news stories.
- Delete your social media apps for 28 days. Then, if you reintroduce them, stay disciplined at times you've designated to view them. There are several effective apps available that can help you lock or block social media apps to enhance productivity and reduce distractions.
- Move the TV out of the bedroom and leave a book on your pillow.
- Go to bed one hour earlier and get up one hour earlier.
- Drink green tea every day.
- Stop eating sugar, starting with breakfast.

- Stop buying ultra-processed foods and dramatically limit your consumption of processed foods.

The path to habit transformation is fraught with challenges. Surmounting the obstacles that stand in our way requires unwavering self-discipline, resilience, determination and even grit. But whether it's overcoming the allure of instant gratification or weathering the storms of setbacks and failures, cultivating resilience is essential for sustaining lasting change.

The impact of habit transformation extends far beyond the confines of individual lives. Like pebbles cast into a pond, the changes we make reverberate outward, influencing those around us and shaping the collective consciousness. By embodying the virtues of health, productivity and positivity, we become beacons of inspiration, causing a ripple effect of transformation that cascades through society.

Who do you want to become, and are your habits in line with the best version of you?

You experience a sense of accomplishment and progress when you consistently engage in good habits. This can boost your self-esteem and happiness as you feel productive and successful. Good habits often form part of a stable routine. Routine provides structure and predictability, which can reduce stress and anxiety, leading to increased happiness. Good habits, such as exercising regularly, eating nutritious foods and getting enough sleep, contribute to better physical health. When your body feels good, it positively impacts your mood and overall wellbeing.

Good habits are often aligned with long-term goals and aspirations. Working towards these goals and seeing progress can bring a sense of fulfilment and happiness. Good habits usually produce positive outcomes, reinforcing the behaviour and creating a positive feedback loop. For example, if you consistently practice gratitude, you may notice improvements in your relationships and overall outlook, enhancing your happiness. Some good habits, such as mindfulness or practising relaxation techniques, can help reduce stress and promote a sense of calm and contentment.

Good habits contribute to elevated happiness by promoting physical and mental wellbeing, fostering a sense of achievement and purpose, and enhancing social connections and overall quality of life.

The importance of changing our habits cannot be overstated. It is through the crucible of habit transformation that we sculpt our destinies and unleash the full potential of our beings. By embracing change, cultivating resilience and harnessing the power of neuroplasticity, we embark on a journey of self-discovery and empowerment. So, let's heed the call to action and dare to tread the path of transformation, for therein lies the promise of a brighter tomorrow.

When you're in the middle of change—real change—it can feel like the ground beneath you is shifting. Old routines fall away, familiar roles dissolve, and you're left standing in a space that feels uncertain, raw and open.

****

This week, try something simple but powerful: observe yourself. Not to judge or fix, but to understand. Notice the small things—how you begin your mornings, how you soothe your discomfort, how you speak to yourself when no one else is around. Ask yourself gently: "Is this a habit I want to carry into the next chapter of my life—or leave behind?"

Then go deeper. Ask:

"If I were on my deathbed right now, would I look back and wish I had done more of this, or less?"

This is not a morbid question. It's a clarifying one. It strips away the noise and brings you back to what's real. In times of change, we often grasp for anything that feels certain. But sometimes what we need most is not to grip harder, but to let go of what no longer serves us.

## REMEMBER THIS

You're in a unique moment right now. Change is a doorway. You get to choose what comes with you and what stays behind. Let this be a week of quiet sorting. Of asking better questions. Of becoming more intentional with your time, your energy and your habits.

Because one day, when you look back, you'll see that the smallest decisions made in uncertain seasons were actually the most defining.

CHAPTER 6

# ALCOHOL: QUIT FOR 12 MONTHS, THEN YOU DECIDE

*Sobriety is not giving up anything. It's a gain, not a loss.*

**Teenage hangover**
There was no hangover. I was energetic the morning after a big night. My recklessness was accepted and even seen as comical by my fellow party animals. What was this new activity that I had found? This new perception of presence and being so in the moment, where nothing else mattered?

The anxiety-reducing effect of drinking alcohol made me feel relaxed and less inhibited, screening any worries about past or future events. This amazing dilution of inhibitions increased my feelings of sociability and my sense of connection and presence.

The bottle's tasty surge of dopamine makes these exciting social experiences feel even more enjoyable and meaningful. My diminished self-consciousness and self-awareness caused me to be less preoccupied with my thoughts and insecurities. I had a newly found confidence to enthusiastically talk to the pretty girl at the party like she was already in love with me.

I loved these new, immediate sensory experiences, the sights, sounds and tactile sensations. They resulted in a heightened sense of presence in the moment, not to mention the addition of amphetamines or hallucinogens.

Drinking with friends gave me this fantastic distortion of time, some blur between moments simultaneously passing more slowly and being over in the blink of an eye. I was having so much fun that the conclusion of one night left me wanting to chase another just like it.

As I slowly sat up, I couldn't help but smile at the memories of last night's epic party with friends. The conversation had flowed as freely as the wine, and all was right with the world for half-a-dozen solid, booze-consuming hours.

But now, as I reached for the bottle of water and the paracetamol on my nightstand, I couldn't ignore the subtle reminders of the night before—a slight headache, a dry mouth, a feeling of lethargy—but I was still capable of another night or two this week, just like the night before.

I was living the days of reckless abandon and carefree indulgence. None of my decisions carried a weight of consequence. I smiled ruefully as I remembered the wild night just gone; the slight hangover was a small price to pay for a good time. Please keep them coming, I say.

**Twenties hangover**

The twenties hangover wasn't quite the enemy yet—it was more of a mild inconvenience, a bump in the road on the long highway of good times. I could wake up with a pounding head and a mouth like sandpaper, but a strong coffee, a cold shower and a bacon-and-egg roll later, I was ready to do it all again. The hangover became part of the ritual, a hazy morning-after badge that proved the night before was worth remembering—or forgetting.

Somewhere between the endless parties, late-night kebabs and sunrise taxi rides, drinking wasn't just a social act anymore—it was a lifestyle. The weekends bled into weekdays, and what was once an occasional blowout became a default way of being. I told myself I was just "living my best years," that this was what your twenties were for—freedom, connection, spontaneity, and stories worth telling.

But there were signs of wear I chose not to see. The hangovers lasted longer. The Monday blues felt heavier. There was a quiet voice somewhere in the background whispering that I was running on borrowed energy, but I drowned it out with another drink. Responsibility was something for future-me to deal with.

Looking back, the twenties hangover was less about the headache and more about the slow, creeping realisation that I was chasing something temporary. Each night out promised connection and belonging, yet I often woke up feeling emptier than before. It was fun—unquestionably fun—but it came with the faintest echo of something unsustainable.

Still, in the blur of youth and bravado, I told myself this was life. The hangover was a small price to pay for being young, wild and free. Tomorrow could wait. The next night out was always calling.

**Thirties hangover**
The pounding in my head matched the relentless beat of the music from last night's party. While my twenties were a blur of late nights and even later mornings, the memories were of fun and enjoyment. This new type of hangover felt particularly brutal. It was starting to feel like I was going through the motions, and these extensive drinking sessions were where the momentum carried me.

You would think my thirties had brought with them a new-found appreciation for moderation, but sometimes old habits die hard. In my twenties, a hangover felt like a badge of honour, proof of a night well spent. But now, as I lay here regretting every sip, I couldn't help but wish to turn back time and make better choices.

Lesson learnt, I thought, as I dragged myself out of bed and reached for a sports drink and aspirin, thinking it would mitigate my wrongdoing. "Never again!"

Gone were the days of bouncing back from a night of heavy drinking with nothing more than some hydration and a greasy breakfast. Now, I had to contend with the reality of being an adult and having real-life responsibilities.

But now, as I nursed my aching head and vowed to take it easy next time, I couldn't help but feel grateful for the wisdom that must proceed as I move into my forties and fifties and settle my drinking habits as children and work responsibilities take centre stage.

No chance of that happening.

**Forties hangover**

You would expect my forties to have brought the sense of wisdom and perspective I had sorely lacked in my thirties. The morning sun filtered through the blinds, casting thin slivers of light across the room. My head felt like it had been stuffed with cotton balls, and every movement sent waves of nausea crashing through me. I groaned and tried to sit up, but my body rebelled against the idea.

The events of last night flashed through my mind like a blurry slideshow: too many shots, too many drinks, too much everything. The taste of those previous drinks still lingered on my tongue, and the memory of dancing wildly and talking rubbish to random people had me cringing.

As I stumbled out of bed and into the bathroom, I saw myself in the mirror. Dark circles under my eyes, hair in disarray, and a complexion that screamed I haven't slept in days. I looked like a walking advertisement for the consequences of excess. Food was hard to stomach, every sip of water felt like a victory, and every noise felt like a dagger to the brain. Hopefully, my kids will be happy on their iPads for the next few hours until my mind can get into first gear.

I swore to myself that I would never drink like that again, but deep down, I knew it was only a matter of time before the next party beckoned.

As I stumbled into the day attempting to be responsible and manage the kid's sporting commitments, I cursed my younger self for thinking I was invincible. Every muscle in my body ached, and the pounding throb in my head threatened to split my skull in two. I gave no consideration to how this bingeing would affect me and those around me.

The fog in my head wouldn't even entirely depart until Thursday. The anxiousness and regret of only doing about 30 per cent of what I wanted to achieve this week were thankfully subsiding. The feeling of being a shit parent for the last few days lingered. At least I was getting my energy back. A drink on Friday night would dull the negative emotions of failing to have any control and self-discipline.

Fuck me. What are my fifties going to be like?

\*\*\*\*

If you can have a couple of drinks or less at a social gathering or have a wine with dinner and then pull up stumps at two, then you have a Jedi gift through genetics or monk-like discipline. If this is you, then you can skip the rest of this chapter. Well done. We will catch up with you in Chapter 5.

If you can't stop at two drinks, then like me (hopefully not as bad), you are powerless against alcohol, and you have to place the wine or beer bottle down for 12 months to experience what the human body with no alcohol genuinely feels like. After a year, make a call on what you want to do next. My goal was 12 months. Life became marginally easier, so I pushed on for another 12 months without wanting to pick up another drink.

If you only have a few drinks a week and are tempted to skip this chapter, let me leave you with one striking fact: research shows that your body can take up to five days to fully recover from just a couple of drinks.

\*\*\*\*

WHOOP—the wearable that tracks performance and recovery—collects billions of data points every single day from its global user base, making it one of the largest and most powerful datasets on human physiology in the world. Dr Kristen Holmes, WHOOP's Global Head of Human Performance and Principal Scientist for the past decade, has had this data at her fingertips. What she and her team have found is eye-opening: when you consume two or more standard alcoholic drinks, it can take five days for critical physiological markers—like heart rate variability (HRV), resting heart rate, respiratory rate and sleep quality—to return to baseline.

This isn't just about shaking off a hangover. It's about a deep, multi-day disruption in how your body regulates essential functions—everything from nervous system balance to sleep architecture. As Dr Holmes explains, "Alcohol consumption has a much longer-lasting impact on health metrics than most people realise. According to extensive WHOOP data, consuming two or more alcoholic drinks affects physiological markers for an average of five days before returning to baseline."

Think about what that means in practice: even moderate drinking—one or two glasses—can compromise your recovery and performance for nearly a week. For people who drink regularly, this creates an overlap effect. If you drink again before your body has fully bounced back, you may never actually give yourself a full recovery window.

A big implication to consider is that this creates a stacking effect. Drinking a few nights a week creates a chronic state of suboptimal recovery, even if you never "feel drunk." The hidden cost isn't just next-day tiredness—it's a measurable decline in resilience, adaptability and long-term health.

Dr Holmes' research is clear: even small amounts of alcohol can profoundly disrupt your ability to recover. For anyone serious about better sleep, stronger performance or genuine health resilience, this is a wake-up call.

So even if you're a Jedi master of moderation, don't dismiss the idea of taking a year off. And if you're more like me—an addict—well, moderation isn't an option. That's why the rest of this chapter is for you.

\*\*\*\*

For the party people out there, there's no denying that booze feels good. The brain releases dopamine and endorphins and instantly gets our buzz on, so we want more. But as the saying goes, alcohol steals happiness from tomorrow.

What goes up must come down. Our brains counteract the effects of alcohol by releasing stress hormones and stimulants like cortisol and norepinephrine. Alcohol affects serotonin, another neurotransmitter linked to mood regulation. Alcohol affects the balance between glutamate (an excitatory neurotransmitter) and GABA (an inhibitory neurotransmitter). Regular bingeing can lead to an overactive glutamate system and a downregulated GABA system, causing increased anxiety and difficulty in experiencing pleasure. The release of these chemicals restores balance, but can lead to a mixed state of stimulation and sedation. This is where increased heart rate, anxiety and a general feeling of unease come into play when the drinks wear off.

Chronic alcohol use, which for a male adult is defined as more than 15 drinks in a week (less for a female), can lead to long-term changes in the brain's chemistry and structure. The brain becomes reliant on alcohol's presence to maintain its balance, and the stress response systems can become overactive. This diminishes the ability to feel pleasure from other activities.

\*\*\*\*

Until my last ski holiday with the kids, I naturally thought I was losing some interest in skiing. The locations we were skiing at were less exciting now, and I needed to look for something new. It felt like all my senses were dulled, failing to respond to the snow like they did years ago. Well, that was the exact issue. It had nothing to do with the snow, the mountains, or my tiring of the activity. It was simply my brain chemistry taking a hit.

My first ski holiday after 13 months without a single drink opened my eyes to the dormant feeling that was always there. In the previous holidays, I was looking through foggy glass; the clarity was missing. As much as it was staring me in the face, it was a moment for me.

Stepping out from the lodge early in the morning after eight hours of sleep, I felt fresh and enthused instead of dusty and broken. The first breath of mountain air is like a baptism. The crispness seized my lungs, filling them with a purity unknown to the lowlands. The scent of pine needles and freshly fallen snow interlaces to create a clean fragrance that seems to erase all remnants of city smog. My shoulders relaxed, the weight of routine slipping away like a discarded coat.

My eyes, initially overwhelmed by the brightness, adjusted to the landscape. The sun is a diamond in a sapphire sky, casting its brilliance over a sea of white. Snowflakes twinkle like tiny, scattered stars, creating a glittering mosaic that seems to stretch into infinity. The slopes I can see on the hill rise majestically, their contours softened by the thick, powdery snow. Tall evergreens, their branches heavy with white, stand like silent sentinels, guarding this winter wonderland. I can see, smell and feel it, and I haven't even clicked into my skis yet. In response to the magical environment I am breathing in around me, my firing sensors release dopamine in my brain.

\*\*\*\*

While half-a-dozen beers the night before are super fun, the fun nights make the world feel much less pleasurable due to having fewer receptors. Before my last holiday, I had become numb, as if all the colour had drained from my life. It wasn't just skiing; I had lost finding pleasure from ordinarily enjoyable activities, leading to a condition known as anhedonia, as the brain's dopamine system becomes desensitised. This desensitisation reduces the ability to feel pleasure from activities that used to be enjoyable.

The good news is that dopamine downregulation isn't permanent. By quitting or even cutting down your drinking to moderate levels, your receptors will start to replenish and restore. This is how I instantly found the complete joy in holidaying in a ski town again. I became un-numb, the colour returned to my world, and the fog had been wiped from the goggles. My quality of life skyrocketed.

\*\*\*\*

When Lou was diagnosed with cancer, I was surprised at how serious the doctors were about alcohol consumption and its detrimental effect on the success of treatment. Her oncologist was steadfast about her avoiding alcohol during treatment to optimise the chances of survival and minimise potential complications.

The doctors told her that her chemotherapy was metabolised by the liver, and alcohol would screw with the metabolism of her medications, potentially reducing their effectiveness or increasing their toxicity. She was told that alcohol suppresses the immune system, increasing the risk of infections and complicating the body's ability to fight cancer and other illnesses. The doctors explained that both cancer treatments and alcohol consumption cause twice the amount of dehydration as usual, along with additional advice that alcohol interferes with the body's ability to absorb nutrients and may worsen nutritional deficiencies. Her doctor told her that the bubbly champagne she thoroughly enjoyed could further strain the liver, potentially leading to liver damage. Alcohol can amplify the side effects of cancer treatments, such as nausea, fatigue and dizziness, making her even sicker than she already was, if that was even possible.

It got me seriously thinking that if alcohol needs to be eliminated for a cancer patient to survive, then it needs to be eliminated for a non-cancer patient to thrive. All for the same reasons:

- Alcohol is a short-term alleviator of feelings of depression, stress or anxiety but, as you know, in the long term it exacerbates these conditions.
- Alcohol affects neurotransmitters in the brain, such as serotonin and dopamine, which play crucial roles in regulating mood. Overconsumption of alcohol disrupts the delicate balance of these neurotransmitters, leading to mood disturbances.
- Alcohol is a diuretic, causing dehydration that contributes to feelings of fatigue and irritability.
- Alcohol fucks with your sleep, even one single drink. It interferes with REM (rapid eye movement) sleep, essential for emotional processing and regulation. Shitty sleep destroys your mood.
- Regular consumption, dysregulates the body's stress response system including the hypothalamic-pituitary-adrenal (HPA)

axis. This dysregulation increases susceptibility to stress and worsens depressive symptoms.
- Getting drunk regularly leads to strained relationships, social isolation and feelings of guilt or shame, all of which contribute to a state far from happiness.
- Prolonged alcohol use leads to structural and functional changes in the brain, including a decreased volume of grey matter and impaired cognitive function. These changes contribute to a negative mood.
- Most of us use alcohol as a maladaptive coping mechanism to deal with stress, anxiety or depression. However, this false reliance on coping can lead to a vicious cycle of continuous, cyclical use and an even worse emotional state.

During COVID-19 isolation periods, I had in-house booze benders about once a fortnight. My daughter was five years old at the time. I thought I was doing this inconspicuously. One morning she asked me, "Dad, can you stop drinking beer?" I only drank about three more times after her request until the feeling of betrayal got the better of me, and I ended my relationship with alcohol.

My brother Tristan gave up alcohol nearly two years before I did, and I could clearly see the difference it made—to his energy, his clarity, his productivity, even his relationships. I still remember telling him, "That's so good you're doing that, but I just can't. My social life and even my work-related commitments just wouldn't allow me to give up drinking entirely." Looking back, it's remarkable how easily we can spin a story to trick our own brains into believing that something meaningful and life-changing simply isn't possible.

Giving up alcohol for a year led to significant changes in my physical, emotional, mental and spiritual wellbeing. Here's a list of what I experienced.

- I wasn't thirsty during the week anymore. Stopping consumption helped my body retain more fluids, improving hydration.
- I experience more restful sleep. This was instant.
- The only place I had ever carried weight was around my tummy. With the reduced alcohol caloric intake, it left in a hurry.
- Initially, I dealt with some mood swings as my body adjusted to the absence of alcohol. Still, I had an instant decrease in anxiety as the depressant effects of alcohol wore off.
- My focus and concentration improved, and my memory was enhanced.
- I stumbled on a clearer perspective on life, promoting a sense of spiritual awakening or clarity that compounded over time.
- My digestive system was working like it should after the recovery from alcohol-induced damage.
- I had increased energy levels as my body no longer had to process all the poison.
- While my sleep improved, I needed less sleep per night than in all the preceding years.
- There was now much more time for other areas and people.
- My emotional states began to stabilise.
- I had significantly more emotional availability for my children, family and friends.
- Enhancing mental clarity has improved my productivity both at work and on personal projects.
- My stress levels plummeted.
- I grew in inner peace as I engaged more with my authentic self.
- My skin looked younger.
- I developed a much stronger immune system and am sick less often, gaining a lot of time.
- I acquired increased self-esteem and confidence.

- My creativity seemed to return.
- Improved physical fitness and endurance.
- Greater emotional resilience and ability to handle stress.
- Increased feelings of happiness and contentment.
- Sharper thinking and problem-solving abilities.
- Improved and increased interest in learning and retaining new information.
- A stronger sense of purpose and direction in my life.
- Increased mindfulness and presence.
- A deepening sense of peace and emotional balance.
- A sense of harmony and alignment with my values.
- Increased emotional fulfilment and satisfaction with my life.
- I have a deeper sense of connection with myself and the world around me.
- Such a better dad. Such a better person.

Several compelling reasons support continuing a life without drinking. I wish I could have a sense of moderation and enjoy the occasional drink, but I can't, so the only alternative was not to drink.

For a long time, alcohol was my escape, a crutch I leaned on to dull the sharp edges of life. But over time, I realised it wasn't just numbing my pain—it was numbing everything. The highs weren't as high, the laughter wasn't as full, and even my love for the people closest to me was muted and distant. My emotional landscape, once vibrant and varied, had shrunk to a narrow strip of flat, grey sameness. I didn't see it happening at first, but looking back, I can see how it stole the richness of my world, leaving me stuck in a place where joy and sorrow were indistinguishable.

I hold zero judgement towards any family member or friend who chooses to drink. My circle of friends are big boozers; they always have been. I prefer not to have an opinion as it's not my hand, glass or mouth. My friends' social and health decisions will not dilute my friendship by .01 per cent. I don't hold any judgement for you either, but hopefully, I have planted a seed in your brain large enough for you to have 12 months free of alcohol so you too can experience the reward.

\*\*\*\*

If you are a big drinker, you may need professional guidance or medical support to help you stop. If you're a heavy drinker and alcohol has ever held power over you, then you already know—it's not something you can manage with moderation. The idea that you can dip your toe back in, just for one harmless drink, is a dangerous illusion. Telling yourself, "I'm in a good place now, I can handle it" is like opening a door you once fought tooth and nail to close. Even left slightly ajar, that door swings wide open, fast. And what waits on the other side is not control or balance, but a 70-degree slope—steep, slick and unforgiving. The moment you step through, even with the best intentions, you're back in the chaos, losing grip and watching your progress unravel. The only way to stay free is to shut the door completely and bolt it. Because for some of us, there's no such thing as just one.

When you shut the door, it gets easier. You will likely experience cravings, especially when you are under stress. You will have to deal with some emotional changes. You will feel like you are missing out. However, it gets easier as the months pass until you relish not being a drinker; you are in charge, and you own it.

\*\*\*\*

Reflect on all the reasons you want to give up alcohol for a year—or forever. Common reasons include health concerns, financial savings, improving relationships and being a better parent.

Write down your clear, concise goal of not drinking for the next 12 months.

Educate yourself! I have given you a bunch of reasons why alcohol is the devil, and I have elaborated on how good I feel and the new life not drinking has given me. Do some research of your own to understand the impact of alcohol on your body and mind, which can strengthen your resolve. Research how alcohol affects physical and mental health, including risks of addiction and long-term diseases. Think about the old people you think drink more than a healthy amount in their lives. How are they looking? How mobile are they? Do you want to be like them?

Find inspiration in the stories of others who have successfully given up alcohol. Plan for challenges, anticipate potential obstacles and prepare strategies to overcome them. Identify triggers by recognising situations, people or emotions that make you want to drink. Develop coping strategies and plan alternative activities or responses for when you face triggers. For instance, go for a walk, call a friend, or engage in a hobby.

Seek support from friends and family. Don't go through this journey alone. Support from others can be crucial. Talk to friends and family, and let them know about your goals so they can provide encouragement and avoid offering you alcohol. A significant one—and the most challenging—is changing your environment by making adjustments to your surroundings that support your new lifestyle. Remove booze from the house and avoid high-risk situations: stay away from places or events where heavy drinking is common, at least initially.

Replacing unhealthy drinking habits with healthier ones can help you maintain your progress. Regular physical activity can improve your mood and reduce stress. Move! Focus on a balanced diet to support overall wellbeing.

Reflect on your journey and celebrate achievements, acknowledge and reward yourself for reaching significant milestones, like one week, one month, six months and then one year of sobriety. Stay motivated and maintain your commitment by staying focused. Keep reminders of your reasons for giving up alcohol where you can see them. Use affirmations to reinforce your decision and boost your confidence.

## REMEMBER THIS

Giving up alcohol is a significant step towards a healthier and more fulfilling life. You can successfully navigate this journey by assessing your habits, setting clear goals, seeking support, and making practical changes. Remember, it's a process that requires patience and persistence, but the rewards are well worth the effort as they are life-changing, and it's all upside.

There's not a soul who's walked away from alcohol and looked back with longing—only with relief, clarity, and an odd kind of peace they never knew they craved. Giving it up is like stepping out of a loud, smoky room into fresh air; your lungs expand, your thoughts sharpen, your mornings come without apology. No one misses the spinning rooms, the slurred truths, the aching regrets. In the silence where the glass used to clink, people find themselves again—steady, unblurred, real. It turns out the real buzz comes not from the bottle, but from waking up to a life you don't need to escape.

CHAPTER 7

# NUTRITION AND FOOD ARE THE BEST MEDICINE

*"Let food be thy medicine and medicine be thy food."*
— *Hippocrates*

The hiss of the can cracks the silence, a sharp exhale of carbonation, as if the Coke itself is eager to escape. Tiny bubbles surge to the surface, fizzing like an excited crowd at a concert. The first sip is electrifying—cold, sharp, and impossibly smooth. A wave of sweetness rushes in, perfectly balanced by the bite of the bubbles. It dances on my tongue, a fleeting thrill; before I know it, my hand moves instinctively for another sip.

The second gulp is even better, the cool burn sliding effortlessly down my throat. It doesn't just quench my thirst—it demands more. The crispness, the tang, the way it lingers just long enough before vanishing, leaving only a craving for the next rush. Each sip fuels a cycle I can't resist. My fingers tighten around the can, condensation slipping against my skin. I try to pace myself, to savour it, but the next thing I know, my head tilts back, and the last golden drop is gone.

I lower the can, surprised and slightly regretful, staring at its empty shell. How did that happen so fast? The taste still lingers, teasing, but the magic is over. The craving is satisfied, but only just. I already want another.

I can't drink a can of Coke (or any other soda) slowly due to a combination of biology, psychology and habit. When I take that first sip, the sugar (or artificial sweeteners) triggers a dopamine release in my brain. Dopamine is the "feel-good" neurotransmitter that reinforces pleasurable behaviours, so with each sip my brain gets a reward, making me want more.

Coke (and all sugary processed foods and drinks) is also designed to be incredibly palatable, with just the right balance of sweetness and acidity. The phosphoric acid slightly dulls my tastebuds, making it easier to keep drinking without feeling overwhelmed by the sugar. The carbonation enhances the experience, stimulating the trigeminal nerve in my mouth and creating a tingling, refreshing sensation that keeps me coming back for more.

My brain associates it with pleasure and refreshment, so once I start drinking, I don't even think about stopping. Even though Coke doesn't hydrate because of its high sugar and sodium content, the cold, fizzy feeling tricks me into thinking it's quenching my thirst, so I keep drinking. Coke is just an example, as Coca-Cola's red-and-white script is probably the world's most recognisable logo and brand. We'll come back to food and drink in a few minutes.

****

The modern-day environment is already stacked against us regarding toxins, causing metabolic dysfunction in our bodies and brains. The abstract from the 2008 paper "Children's Environmental Health: Intergenerational Equity in Action – A Civil Society Perspective" by Mariann Lloyd-Smit and Bro Sheffield-Brotherton will tell you that.

Since World War II, approximately 80,000 new commercial synthetic chemicals have been released into the environment, with approximately 1500 new chemicals released annually. Most of these have not been adequately tested for their impacts on human health or their particular impacts on children and the developing fetus. Yet, children are exposed to hazardous chemicals through residues in their food, indoor and outdoor air pollution, and household products, as well as contaminated house dust. Many of these synthetic chemicals are persistent and bio-accumulative, remaining in the human body long after exposure. Fetuses developing in the womb acquire toxic chemicals that have bioaccumulated in the mother's body and readily cross the placental barrier. Babies are now born with many man-made chemicals in their tiny bodies. Newborns take in more of these toxic chemicals through breast milk or formula. There are no tests to assess the combined impacts of the "chemical soup" to which children are exposed. WHO, UNICEF and UNEP have reported a growing number of children's health impacts caused by exposure to hazardous chemicals, including asthma, birth defects, hypospadias, behavioural disorders, learning disabilities, autism, cancer, dysfunctional immune systems, neurological impairments, and reproductive disorders. WHO states that approximately 3 million children under the age of five die every year due to environmental hazards, and this is not limited to developing countries. All children in the developing and developed world are affected by exposure to hazardous chemicals. In 2004, the European Union's Ministerial Conference on Children's Environmental Health identified air pollution, unsafe water conditions, and lead exposure as the main culprits in the deaths and disabilities of children in Europe. The conference found that by reducing exposure to hazardous chemicals, the lives of many children could be saved. The key issues in children's environmental health and potential policy and management remedies are examined from national (Australian) and international perspectives.

It's been eye-opening to learn more about the chemicals we are exposed to in everyday life, often without realising their potential risks. In household and consumer products, formaldehyde is commonly found in furniture, pressed wood and cosmetics, leading to respiratory issues and cancer. Bisphenol A (BPA), present in plastics and the linings of food cans, disrupts hormones and affects reproductive health. Phthalates, used in plastics, personal care products and fragrances, also act as endocrine disruptors. Triclosan, an antimicrobial found in soaps and toothpaste, has been linked to antibiotic resistance and hormone imbalances. Additionally, per- and polyfluoroalkyl substances (PFAS), commonly used in non-stick cookware, waterproof clothing and food packaging, have been associated with cancer and immune suppression.

In food and beverages, pesticides such as glyphosate are commonly found in non-organic produce and grains, posing risks to cancer and hormone disruption (There is more information on this chemical on the next page). Sodium nitrite and nitrate, present in processed meats, have been linked to cancer, while artificial sweeteners like aspartame and saccharin, commonly found in diet sodas and sugar-free products, raise concerns about possible carcinogenic effects.

Air and environmental exposure also contribute to chemical risks. Benzene, released from petrol/gasoline, cigarette smoke and industrial emissions, has been linked to leukaemia and bone marrow damage. Particulate matter (PM2.5 and PM10), which is found in air pollution from vehicles, wildfires and industrial sources, contributes to the development of lung and heart diseases. Radon, a naturally occurring radioactive gas found in homes, is a leading cause of lung cancer in non-smokers. At the same time, asbestos, once widely used in insulation and still present older buildings, can lead to mesothelioma and lung disease.

Water contaminants further increase health risks. Lead, commonly found in old pipes and paint, causes severe neurological damage, particularly in children. Mercury, present in some fish and industrial pollution, affects the nervous system, while arsenic, which contaminates groundwater in certain regions, has been linked to cancer and organ damage.

Finally, workplace and industrial exposure introduce additional hazards. Toluene, found in paint thinners, nail polish and industrial solvents, hurts the nervous system. Ammonia, used in cleaning products, can cause lung irritation and burns, while chlorine, commonly used in disinfectants and pool cleaners, may lead to irritation of the lungs and skin.

Unfortunately, these chemicals have become part of daily life. It is in our best interests to minimise exposure in any way possible. This is often easier said than done. In my opinion, product choices are the best place to start.

\*\*\*\*

Let's examine one chemical related to food and beverages that frequently appears in my discovery reading, which I briefly mentioned before: glyphosate. If you haven't heard of this, it won't take much research to find that glyphosate is a broad-spectrum systemic herbicide used to kill weeds, especially annual broadleaf weeds and grasses that compete with crops. It is also used to dry out crops, making them easier to harvest. It was discovered by Monsanto chemist John E Franz in 1970 and brought to market under the trade name Roundup in 1974. Glyphosate works by inhibiting a specific enzyme pathway, the shikimic acid pathway, which is necessary for plants and some microorganisms. Glyphosate has been registered for use in Australia for over 40 years. Around 500 glyphosate products are registered by the Australian Pesticides and Veterinary Medicines Authority (APVMA).

Many of our crops that make their way to the kitchen appear to contain glyphosate. Primarily from crops where the chemical is used for weed control or as a desiccant (substance used to induce or sustain a state of dryness (desiccation) in its vicinity before harvest). Some foods that have a very high probability of containing glyphosate include:

- Grain: wheat, oats, barley, and rye
- Cereal products: bread, pasta, cereals, and crackers
- Legumes: soybeans, chickpeas, lentils, and peas
- Fruits and vegetables: apples, oranges, and potatoes
- Processed foods: foods made with ingredients from glyphosate-treated crops

The International Agency for Research on Cancer (IARC), a part of the World Health Organization (WHO), classified glyphosate as "probably carcinogenic to humans" (Group 2A) in 2015. Some studies suggest that glyphosate may act as an endocrine disruptor, affecting hormone balance and potentially leading to reproductive issues and developmental problems. Glyphosate has antimicrobial properties and may contribute to antibiotic resistance by affecting the microbiomes of soil, plants, animals and humans. Some studies and legal cases have linked glyphosate exposure to non-Hodgkin lymphoma and other cancers. Glyphosate exposure has been associated with reduced fertility, birth defects and other reproductive problems. Animal studies have shown that glyphosate can cause liver and kidney damage. Evidence suggests that glyphosate can impair immune function, potentially increasing susceptibility to infections and autoimmune diseases. Glyphosate may disrupt the gut microbiota, leading to digestive issues and potentially contributing to conditions like inflammatory bowel disease.

Research conducted by Washington State University (WSU) has found that glyphosate exposure in pregnant rats can lead to significant health issues in their offspring, persisting into the third generation. The study demonstrated that although the initial generation showed no apparent adverse effects, the second and third generations experienced various health problems. These included increases in prostate, kidney, and ovarian diseases, obesity and birth abnormalities.

Specifically, third-generation male rats showed a 30% increase in prostate disease, while third-generation female rats exhibited a 40% increase in kidney disease. Additionally, more than a third of the second-generation mothers had unsuccessful pregnancies, and a significant proportion of third-generation rats were obese. The study, published in *Scientific Reports*, suggests that epigenetic changes are the underlying mechanism. These changes, triggered by environmental factors like glyphosate, can turn genes on or off, leading to health issues that can be passed down through generations.

And how about this to make things interesting? There is evidence to suggest that glyphosate can be found in rainwater samples. Several studies have reported the presence of glyphosate and its degradation product, aminomethylphosphonic acid (AMPA), in various environmental compartments, including rainwater. The USGS has conducted studies that detected glyphosate in rainwater across the Midwest of the USA. For example, a 2011 study found glyphosate in approximately 60% to 100% of rainwater and air samples collected in agricultural areas during the growing season.

Research conducted in Europe has also reported the presence

of glyphosate in rainwater. A study in Germany found glyphosate in 40% of rainwater samples collected over a year. Glyphosate can enter the atmosphere through volatilisation and wind erosion after being applied to crops. Once airborne, it can be transported over long distances and deposited back to the ground via precipitation. The presence of glyphosate in rainwater raises concerns about its potential impacts on non-target plants and aquatic ecosystems. Even at low concentrations, repeated exposure through rainfall can lead to the accumulation of pollutants in the environment. The detection of glyphosate in rainwater underscores the widespread use of this herbicide and its ability to travel through the environment, potentially leading to significant ecological implications.

Despite the numerous concerns outlined here, regulatory agencies such as the Environmental Protection Agency (EPA) in the US and the European Food Safety Authority (EFSA) have deemed glyphosate safe when used according to label directions. Some may argue that it's not as toxic as the evidence suggests, but countries like Belgium, France and the Netherlands have banned its household use, and Germany, widely known as the house of chemicals, plans to ban it too. Although I only highlighted this one chemical among the 20 I briefly mentioned, it's concerning that many people consume this herbicide on a daily basis.

\*\*\*\*

Do you often wonder why everyone around you seems to be getting sick? I assume we all ponder why so many of my friends and family have had or do have cancer. We spend most of our lives trying to avoid falling pregnant, and then it feels like the majority can't fall pregnant when we want to. This was certainly the case for Lou and me as we tried for years before turning to IVF. Are more people having heart attacks? Are more people getting dementia? I'm sure

I am not the only one who thinks this every time another person in my life has a health issue.

We are paddling uphill to survive, and many of the population are not surviving. And while chemicals like glyphosate may be present in food, I haven't yet discussed food itself.

The reason I have painted a dark picture is to think about these things, and now add the damage we choose to inflict on ourselves through sugar and ultra-processed foods. We make conscious decisions to consume food, wreaking havoc not just on ourselves but also causing epidemics worldwide.

\*\*\*\*

Let's talk about sugar first.

I have always loved sugar—you name it: lollies, cake, chocolate and soda. When I gave up drinking alcohol on 16 December 2022, I increased my sugar binges to fill the void. I was reaping the alcohol-free benefits of feeling fresh, and my productivity increased exponentially. Still, it wasn't until I gave up sugar in July 2023 that my health and feeling good skyrocketed.

Sugar may not be classified as a poison, but it behaves like one. Sugar is made up of glucose and fructose molecules, and our bodies then break it down. When you metabolise fructose in excess, your liver has no choice but to turn that energy into liver fat, and that liver fat causes all of the downstream metabolic diseases. Sugar is directly linked to a multitude of health issues, including mental health problems, inflammation, gut dysbiosis and insulin resistance.

Diets rich in added sugars have been associated with mood disorders. This connection can be partly attributed to sugar's impact on the brain. High sugar consumption can lead to fluctuations in blood glucose levels, which can result in mood swings, irritability and fatigue. Additionally, sugar can affect the regulation of neurotransmitters. For instance, serotonin, a neurotransmitter that regulates mood, can be disrupted by high-sugar diets, contributing to feelings of depression and anxiety.

The human gut microbiome, a complex community of microorganisms in the digestive tract, plays a crucial role in overall health. A balanced microbiome supports digestion, nutrient absorption and immune function. However, high-sugar diets can disrupt this balance, leading to a condition known as gut dysbiosis. Excessive sugar promotes the growth of harmful bacteria and yeast while inhibiting the growth of beneficial bacteria. This imbalance can lead to gastrointestinal issues, including bloating, constipation and diarrhoea. Moreover, gut dysbiosis has been linked to broader health problems, including obesity, diabetes and even mental health disorders.

Insulin resistance is a precursor to type 2 diabetes and is characterised by the body's diminished ability to respond to insulin, a hormone that regulates blood sugar levels. Consuming high amounts of sugar, especially fructose, can lead to insulin resistance. When the body is frequently exposed to high sugar levels, the pancreas produces more insulin to manage the blood sugar levels. Over time, cells become less responsive to insulin, resulting in higher blood sugar levels and, ultimately, the development of type 2 diabetes. Insulin resistance is also associated with other metabolic conditions such as obesity, non-alcoholic fatty liver disease and metabolic syndrome.

Chronic inflammation plays a crucial role in various diseases, including cardiovascular disease, diabetes and cancer. Excessive sugar intake has been shown to promote inflammation in the body. When sugar is consumed in large amounts, it can cause an increase in the production of inflammatory cytokines, proteins that regulate the immune response. This inflammatory response can lead to tissue damage and contribute to the development of chronic diseases. Moreover, high sugar consumption can exacerbate conditions like arthritis, where inflammation is already a significant issue. Inflammation was the drawcard that drew my attention to all of sugar's negative impacts.

I ate healthily 80 per cent of the time, so I didn't acknowledge how detrimental consuming sugar was—even though I thought I was doing it in moderation. Physical reasons were initially the catalyst for reducing my sugar consumption. I hadn't been able to run for 18 months because of injuries, three of which were patella tendonitis, peroneal tendonitis and plantar fasciitis. Overuse, sporting accidents and repetitive stress most probably caused these issues with my lower limbs. However, when I read about injuries and rehabilitation options, inflammation was common across these types of injuries. Inflammation is a shared thread in many ailments, so I embarked on a research tangent to explore where else sugar might be causing potential harm, both now and in the years to come.

Naively, I was surprised to learn that inflammation is linked to multiple major diseases. Cardiovascular diseases, such as atherosclerosis, can lead to heart attacks and strokes. Rheumatoid arthritis, an autoimmune disease, causes inflammation in the joints. Inflammatory bowel disease (IBD), which includes Crohn's disease and ulcerative colitis, is characterised by inflammation of the gastrointestinal tract. Inflammation of the airways is seen in asthma (which I've had since childhood), leading to breathing difficulties, and in chronic obstructive pulmonary disease (COPD). Plenty of people I know have many of these issues.

Autoimmune diseases, such as lupus, multiple sclerosis and psoriasis, involve inflammation where the immune system mistakenly attacks healthy tissues. As mentioned, chronic low-grade inflammation is linked to insulin resistance and the development of type 2 diabetes. Obesity, particularly excess visceral fat, can lead to chronic inflammation. This condition also increases the risk of various cancers, including colorectal, liver and pancreatic cancers. Inflammation in the brain is thought to play a role in neurodegenerative diseases like Alzheimer's. Persistent inflammation can cause damage to the kidneys over time, ultimately leading to chronic kidney disease. Periodontitis involves inflammation of the gums and supporting structures of the teeth.

Other health issues related to inflammation include hayfever, eczema and food allergies. Sinusitis, an inflammation of the sinuses, can become a chronic condition. Inflammatory myopathies are a group of diseases causing muscle inflammation and weakness. Fibromyalgia, characterised by widespread pain and fatigue, is believed to be linked to inflammation. Chronic fatigue syndrome may also involve inflammation, which contributes to persistent fatigue.

Sugar plays a significant role in triggering inflammation, particularly when consumed in excess. I was utterly ignorant of the fact that the body processes "white" foods like bread and pasta similarly to sugar because they are made from refined carbohydrates that break down quickly into glucose. When consumed, these refined carbs are rapidly digested and absorbed into the bloodstream, causing a spike in blood sugar levels similar to that of sugar. This gives the pancreas another incentive to release more insulin, which, as we've seen, can lead to insulin resistance and further inflammation.

Let's add ultra-processed food into the mix, as nine out of ten people I know consume a daily diet that includes these foods. Ultra-processed food is the exact opposite of nutrient-dense food. Due to their composition and effects on the body, processed foods are often linked to various adverse health outcomes. They are a major contributor to nutritional deficiencies due to their low nutrient density. These foods typically lack essential nutrients, such as vitamins, minerals and fibre, and are often high in calories but low in nutritional value. As a result, they can lead to deficiencies if they make up a significant part of one's diet.

One of the primary concerns with processed foods is their high added sugar content, which, as we've seen, can lead to numerous health issues. Furthermore, processed foods often contain unhealthy fats, including trans fats and highly saturated fats. Trans fats are particularly harmful as they raise low-density lipoprotein (LDL) levels while lowering high-density lipoprotein (HDL), increasing the risk of heart disease.

Another issue is the high sodium content in processed foods, which is used to enhance flavour and preserve shelf life. Excessive salt intake is associated with increased blood pressure, a significant risk factor for heart disease and stroke. Additionally, processed foods contain chemical additives and preservatives to improve flavour, texture and shelf life. Some of these additives, such as artificial colourings and flavourings, can cause adverse reactions in some people and may pose long-term health risks. Preservatives like nitrates and nitrites (also found in many processed meats), while preventing spoilage, have been linked to an increased risk of cancer. The consumption of processed foods is also linked to an increased risk of chronic diseases. Their high-calorie content and low nutritional value can contribute to overeating and weight gain.

Processed foods often have low fibre content. Fibre is essential for digestive health and a lack of fibre can lead to constipation and other digestive issues. Fibre also plays a crucial role in regulating blood sugar levels and reducing cholesterol. High consumption of processed foods can negatively impact the gut microbiota, the beneficial bacteria in the digestive system, which in turn affects overall health, including immune function and mental wellbeing. Diets high in processed foods have been linked to an increased risk of mood disorders, such as depression and anxiety, as poor nutrition can affect brain function and mood regulation. Eating a diet high in processed foods from a young age can have lifelong health consequences, setting the stage for chronic diseases later in life.

I'm incredibly fortunate that my super-active, healthy, 75-year-old parents have been hyper-conscious of what should be on the end of my fork my whole life. However, I went to boarding school from the start of high school and then straight to college, followed by house-sharing with friends, so I have had to manage my diet since I was 12 years old. For the most part, I have done an okay job.

As I said at the start of the chapter, I had this 80/20 rule that I applied for most of this time: If 80% of the food I consumed is "healthy", then the 20% won't make a difference to my overall health. When I decided to eliminate sugar and processed foods from my diet and increase the nutrition my body needed, I realised that my 80/20 rule was flawed. You may be able to get away with a false 80/20 rule in your youth, but it catches up with you fast as your metabolism slows down and you become less active.

The primary catalysts for focusing on my diet were first based on something other than increasing my happiness. It was my inflammation issues, most likely due to old sporting injuries, my age and poor injury management. I needed to put a system in place for the healthy 90-year-old I envisioned and accomplish the 50by50 physical goals on my list. If inflammation through diet contributed to my ailments or prevented me from healing, I was motivated to fix it. I started reading books on diet and following social profiles of people with rhetoric that I needed to hear.

If you want to follow the social posts, podcast and books of some of the key influences that I have enjoyed, the following wisdom is a great place to start:

Dr Mark Hyman
Dr Rangan Chatterjee
Rich Roll
Dr Rhonda Patrick
Dr Andrew Huberman
Dr Gabrielle Lyon

I am well aware that not just lifestyle, diet and environmental exposure cause inflammation. Genetic predisposition may also play a role. However, I wanted to cover every possible base to help me heal and run again. Being asthmatic, having eczema at times, and having a fear of developing CTE (chronic traumatic encephalopathy) because of my multiple concussions, and having a wife who died of cancer have all been additional motivators to increase healthspan for my kids and me. I was motivated to reduce any inflammation in my body and brain.

Managing inflammation involves addressing underlying factors through lifestyle changes and dietary adjustments, and medical treatment should not be ruled out if needed. However, from what I have observed, medical treatment often treats the symptoms and not the cause, while lifestyle changes and dietary adjustments treat the cause and have a halo effect on your whole physiological being.

****

Before I made any dietary changes, my chronological aging body was slowing down and screaming for help, and it was living proof of what the science I was reading said. Not getting enough essential nutrients, such as vitamins, minerals and omega-3 fatty acids, affected my brain chemistry and overall health. Deficiencies directly impacted my mood and contributed to subpar happiness. Eating processed foods and sugars daily was causing spikes and crashes in my blood sugar levels, leading to fluctuations in energy levels and making me tired and lethargic. The processed foods combined with all the unhealthy fats and excessive sugar were causing inflammation throughout my body, contributing to many of my physical injuries and prolonging my rehabilitation. My digestive system was out of whack as the balance of bacteria in my gut was leading to digestive issues. It negatively impacted my overall wellbeing and happiness.

My gut is currently a focus of mine, and I am researching my options to maximise its potential. When I read that approximately 90% of the body's serotonin is produced in the gut, it provided instant motivation to link improvement in my gut health to my overall happiness. This connection underscores the significance of gut health in shaping my mood, mental wellbeing and overall health.

While my body suffered, it was not until I felt the physical benefit of food as medicine that I realised how the brain relies on a steady supply of nutrients to function optimally. When I wasn't consuming the right fuel, my cognitive function suffered, affecting my ability to concentrate, solve problems and regulate my emotions.

Dietary adjustments play a significant role in managing inflammation. Consuming anti-inflammatory foods, such as fruits and vegetables rich in antioxidants and phytochemicals, can help reduce inflammation. Healthy fats, such as omega-3 fatty acids found in fatty fish, flaxseeds, chia seeds, walnuts and olive oil, have anti-inflammatory properties. Wholegrains such as brown rice, quinoa, oats and wholewheat products, which contain fibre and nutrients, also help reduce inflammation. Incorporating herbs and spices like turmeric, ginger, garlic and cinnamon into meals can further reduce inflammation.

I have a list of the following foods, along with images of them, visible in the kitchen: olive oil, green tea, mushrooms, broccoli, berries, turmeric, avocado, capsicum, fatty fish and bone broth. I buy more of these than ever, and I have consumed more in the last 12 months than in the preceding 10 years.

It is essential to avoid processed foods high in trans fats, refined sugars and additives, as they can contribute to increased inflammation. Consuming sugary beverages, refined carbohydrates such as white bread and pastries, and processed meat should be limited. Staying well hydrated by drinking plenty of water throughout the day supports optimal body function and reduces inflammation. A balanced diet rich in various nutrients, focusing on wholefoods, is vital. Reducing sodium intake by avoiding processed foods, using herbs and spices for flavouring and moderating caffeine consumption can help reduce inflammation. By making these dietary adjustments, you can effectively manage and reduce inflammation, promoting overall health and wellbeing.

After watching Dan Buettner's work on Blue Zones, reading *Ikigai: The Japanese Secret to a Long and Happy Life*, written by Héctor García and Francesc Miralles, and reading two of Dr Mark Hyman's books, I started experimenting further with my diet to see what works best for me.

At the time of writing this chapter, I'm still experimenting and learning what works best. Everyone is different, and different diets have varying effects on different people.

I have people all around me who seem to be thriving on their specific diet. I have a friend who is on a carnivore diet; he's in his fifties and looks, and acts like an energetic 30-year-old.

My dad settled on a Mediterranean diet focusing on fruits, vegetables, whole grains, legumes, nuts and seeds. These foods provide a rich array of vitamins, minerals, antioxidants and fibre. The diet also encourages the consumption of healthy fats, primarily from sources like olive oil and fatty fish. These fats are rich in omega-3 fatty acids, which have anti-inflammatory properties and are beneficial for heart and brain health. For the most part, a Mediterranean diet is moderate in protein intake with moderate amounts of lean protein sources, such as fish, poultry and legumes, while limiting red meat consumption. He thrives on this diet. If you saw how healthy, happy, positive and active he was, you would be like, "I'm having what he's having."

My mum is on a wholefood, pescatarian and plant-based diet that emphasises natural, unprocessed foods, with close to zero consumption of refined sugar, dairy and processed products, instead promoting fruits, vegetables, legumes, wholegrains, nuts and seeds as dietary staples. Fermented foods, such as sauerkraut, are recommended for promoting gut health, and she emphasises the importance of drinking plenty of water.

I have a friend on a ketogenic diet. She's following the advice from Dr Georgia Ede and her book, *Change Your Diet, Change Your Mind*. I have read this book and it's thought-provoking. If you or your child has autism or severe ADD, I would add this book to your reading list. Dr Ede details how changing your diet can significantly impact your mental health, as the food you consume influences brain chemistry and emotional wellbeing. Regardless of the diet you follow, after reading this book, you will become well aware of the key points I have been advocating for: that diets high in refined carbohydrates and ultra-processed foods can lead to inflammation and oxidative stress, which are linked to mood disorders and cognitive decline.

I tested a vegetarian diet for a while, setting up my controlled environment and eating no meat for six months. I felt good on this diet, but I also lost some muscle mass and strength as a result. I reintroduced red meat into my diet, focusing on grass-fed, high-quality beef and eliminating all processed meat. I have found a middle ground where I feel good and have increased strength.

I am continuing to work on finding the perfect balance for my physical and mental health through my diet, but cutting out sugar and processed foods has been the most significant change for me, and it has yielded the most favourable outcome. Lifestyle changes and dietary adjustments are within your control. It does take massive willpower, but it's in your control.

****

The single most consistent thread I've observed across all genuinely healthy diets—whether Mediterranean, paleo, plant-based or low-carb—is the elimination of sugar and ultra-processed foods. These two elements are the common denominators of poor health outcomes, and removing them is the most powerful first step you can take towards transformation. Forget fads and quick fixes—this is the foundation.

When you cut out added sugars and processed junk, you're not just changing what's on your plate. You're resetting your biology. Cravings diminish, energy stabilises, sleep improves and inflammation subsides. Mental clarity returns. Your gut microbiome begins to flourish. The body, remarkably resilient, starts to heal.

If you do nothing else but remove sugar and ultra-processed foods, you are already more than halfway towards radically improved physical and mental health. This is not about deprivation—it's about liberation. Begin here, and the rest of the path becomes infinitely easier to walk.

## Tips on how to give up sugar and processed foods

Just don't buy it.

Reduce the temptation and refrain from buying it.

It's challenging at the start, but it gets easier with time.

Eliminate sugar, ultra-processed foods, glycaemic foods, refined wheat flour, a lot of your gluten intake, and all liquid sugar calories. Your body is the most competent doctor; make changes and see how you feel. If you get the same benefits that I did, simply getting out of bed in the morning or picking yourself up off the floor will become significantly easier.

If you add these items to your shopping basket, then stop.

1. **Sugary breakfast cereals**
   Contain refined grains, sugar and artificial flavours.
   Marketed as healthy, but often lacking essential nutrients.
2. **Soft drinks and energy drinks**
   High in added sugars or artificial sweeteners.

Provide empty calories with no nutritional benefit.
3. **Packaged snack foods**
   Includes chips, pretzels and flavoured crackers.
   Often fried, salty and made with refined oils.
4. **Instant noodles and soups**
   High in sodium, artificial flavours and preservatives.
   Low in nutritional value.
5. **Processed meats**
   Sausages, hot dogs, bacon and deli meats.
   Contain nitrates, high salt levels and other additives.
6. **Frozen ready meals**
   Includes pizzas, TV and pre-cooked dinners.
   Often high in unhealthy fats, sodium and preservatives.
7. **Confectionery and candy**
   Loaded with refined sugars, artificial flavours and colours.
   Minimal to no nutritional benefit.
8. **Packaged bread and baked goods**
   Includes white bread, muffins and cakes.
   Made with refined flour, added sugars and preservatives.
9. **Flavoured yoghurts and desserts**
   Often high in added sugars and artificial ingredients.
   Marketed as healthy, but can lack protein and natural probiotics.
10. **Fast food items**
    Burgers, fries and fried chicken.
    Deep-fried, calorie-dense and high in unhealthy fats and sodium.

Look up "food" in the dictionary, and the result will be "any nourishing substance that is eaten, drunk, or otherwise taken into the body to sustain life, provide energy, promote growth, etc." Unfortunately, most of the shelf space at your local supermarket doesn't fit this definition, so be wise.

Our bodies are like cars, finely tuned machines crafted with precision and care. When new, they gleam with vitality, every part in perfect sync, running smoothly with little need for attention. The engine purrs, the tyres easily grip the road, and the miles glide effortlessly by.

However, as the years pass, even best-made vehicle begins to show signs of wear. The engine might sputter, paint fades, and once-fluid motions can become stiff and laboured. Like an old car, our bodies need regular maintenance to run smoothly.

Imagine an old classic, a car that has seen the world and has stories etched into every scratch and dent. With regular servicing, oil changes, tyre rotations and the occasional part replacement, that car can continue to run, each mile adding to its rich history. Neglect it, however, and it will break down, leaving its potential untapped and its journey unfinished.

Our bodies are much the same. They can continue to serve us well beyond their prime with proper care and attention. This means regular exercise to keep the engine strong, a balanced diet to fuel our journey, and routine check-ups to catch any issues before they become serious problems. Cut out the sugar and processed foods, which are the equivalent of low-grade fuel that clogs the engine and wears down its parts, and replace them with nutritious, wholesome alternatives. Your body will thank you, running smoothly and efficiently, the odometer ticking towards a century and beyond.

Picture yourself as the driver of this remarkable vehicle: each decision you make is a turn of the wheel, each healthy habit a pit stop that keeps you on the road. The open highway stretches out before you, filled with endless possibilities. With the proper care, your journey will be long, your experiences rich, and your final destination a place of fulfilment and satisfaction.

So treat your body like the valuable vehicle it is. Keep it well-maintained, fuelled with the best nutrients, and driven with purpose and care. Your life's road trip is a grand adventure, and with the proper upkeep, you'll be cruising down the highway of health, happy and flourishing for many miles to come.

Since refining my own fuel by removing sugar and processed foods, my body and mind have found a new rhythm. Clarity has replaced fog. My mood feels balanced, my thoughts calm and steady. Sleep comes easily now, and I wake with a quiet vitality that carries me smoothly through the day, no longer caught in the jarring stops and starts of energy highs and crashes. My joints and muscles move with a freedom I haven't felt in fifteen years, and even long-held companions like asthma and eczema have eased their grip. It's extraordinary how the right nourishment can tune the whole system, transforming not just how you move through the world, but how the world feels as you move through it.

## How does this link to Stoicism?

I see a strong connection between a good diet and Stoicism, as both emphasise self-discipline, moderation and living in accordance with reason. When I think about Stoic principles, like those taught by Seneca and Epictetus, I realise how much self-control plays a role in maintaining a healthy diet. Avoiding overeating, processed foods and indulgent cravings requires the same kind of restraint that Stoicism encourages in all aspects of life. Living in harmony with reason also resonates with me, reminding me to choose whole, natural foods over artificial or highly processed options.

Stoicism teaches me to be indifferent to fleeting pleasures and to avoid being ruled by desires. This mindset enables me to approach food with mindfulness, viewing it as nourishment rather than a means of emotional comfort. I also appreciate how the Stoics valued endurance and resilience, often practising voluntary discomfort, like fasting or eating simple meals, to strengthen their discipline. Applying this to my life, I see how making rational, health-focused choices in my diet builds physical wellbeing and mental strength.

A modern Stoic-inspired diet means prioritising simplicity and nourishment. I aim to embrace wholefoods, mindful eating and even intermittent fasting, which I experiment with as I write this chapter. When I view food as fuel rather than an indulgence, I feel more in control and aligned with Stoic ideals.

The food choices we make—whether it's a quick snack from a convenience store, an entire grocery haul or our daily meals—directly impact our health, energy levels and overall wellbeing. When hunger strikes, especially when we're unprepared, we often reach for whatever is most convenient—packaged chips, chocolate bars or sugary drinks—without considering the long-term consequences. These impulse purchases are usually high in sugar, unhealthy fats and refined carbs, which lead to energy crashes, cravings, inflammation in the body and much worse.

What goes into our shopping trolley plays a significantly more important role. If our carts are filled with processed foods, sodas and quick-fix meals, that's exactly what we'll eat at home. Instead, we need to shift our focus to whole, nutrient-dense foods—fresh fruits and vegetables, lean proteins, healthy fats and wholegrains. Making intentional choices at the grocery store ensures that we have better options available when hunger strikes.

## REMEMBER THIS

Ultimately, what we put in our mouths reflects our habits and the decisions we make. If we continue to fuel our bodies with processed and sugary foods, we will experience sluggishness, weight gain and potentially long-term health issues. But if we consciously change our approach—choosing real, nourishing foods—we can improve our energy, digestion and mental clarity.

The change begins today, with small but deliberate choices that can ultimately transform your health.

CHAPTER 8

# MOVE—USE IT OR LOSE IT

*"We don't stop playing because we grow old;
we grow old because we stop playing."*
*– George Bernard Shaw*

Remember, you have the power to shape your future. You need to create a vision of yourself many years from now to reach your intended destination. You should have a future vision or visions that cover the five dimensions of health: physical, mental, emotional, spiritual and social. They are all deeply connected, but movement and exercise are bodily, so let's focus our attention there.

In Chapter 5, I mentioned that for me, the spark for change was simply the vision I had for myself 30 years from now. My most vivid future vision is teaching my grandchildren to ski and adventure in the back country. I'm an extremely passionate skier; I love the sport. For me, it's a flow state like no other. Standing at the precipice, my breath forming wisps of vapour in the crisp air, my skis slicing through the virgin snow like a bird taking flight. Every turn is a symphony of motion, a dance between gravity and grace. It is a moment when nothing else matters but the pure, unadulterated joy of skiing through untracked white terrain. In the realm of deep, powdery snow there are no boundaries, no limitations—only endless possibilities and boundless freedom. I have gratefully shared this feeling with Noah and Evie, and I will do the same for their children. I want to take my grandkids away skiing for days and manage it alone if my children are busy with work or need a break. I want to do this with abundant energy and ability.

I choose to spend very little time away from my children. Still, as I'm writing this chapter on a plane this very minute, my parents are enthusiastically managing Noah and Evie for the week so I can compete in a 480-kilometre motorcycle desert race out of Alice Springs, called The Finke. My parents walked 100 kilometres over six days last week, from Collioure in France to Cadaques in Spain along the Costa Brava. After the walk and some time in Italy, they flew home, had a weekend to recover from their jet lag, and then went straight into caring for my beautiful little rascals so I could cleanse my brain and reset my soul in the desert. If your parents are doing that and it isn't enough motivation to go and get after it, then I don't know what it is.

If my children have kids at 35, and I start skiing with my grandchildren when they are five, I will be 75. When I'm chronologically 75 (this can't be altered in any way, shape or form), my biological age (based on physiological evidence, how old my cells and tissues are) will be 55; that's the goal.

The technology behind biological age testing is continually improving. Science assesses how well your body is aging based on various factors, including lifestyle, genetics and overall health. The tests are conducted using age calculators and fitness assessments, where biomarkers associated with aging are measured, including cholesterol levels, blood sugar levels, inflammation markers and telomere length. Telomeres are the protective caps at the end of chromosomes, and their length is associated with aging. You can also undergo DNA methylation tests, which analyse patterns of DNA methylation to estimate biological age. Methylation is an epigenetic modification that affects gene expression and can change with age.

****

I am currently 47 years old in chronological terms; my biological fitness age is 42, which is five years younger, achieved through two years of concentrated effort. I will extend this even further as good habits compound.

I've had people my whole life tell me, "You're going to be a cripple when you're older!" "All these injuries you've sustained will return and haunt you!" People have reason to believe this, and only three years ago I would have agreed with them.

As a school athlete and rugby player, I ran so much that overuse and poor maintenance have severely affected various bones, tendons, ligaments, joints and cartilage. Rugby is a collision sport, so years of games and training can take a toll on your body. I've had my fair share of high-impact injuries off the field, too, where my travelling inertia on skis or a motorcycle abruptly ended with solid ground or a not-so-forgiving tree.

To start at my feet:
I have broken my little toe.
I fractured my heel.
Twisted ankles that saw foot swelling as big as a workboot.
I have dealt with chronic shin splints and patella tendonitis.
A syndesmosis injury to my left lower leg.
I've torn the meniscus in both knees.
Grade one, two and three medial tears.
I have been sidelined for weeks with quadricep and hamstring tears. I once heard my hamstring tear while running down the sideline of the rugby field with the ball in hand.
I've had four transverse process spinal fractures.
Separation of the shoulder with an AC injury.
I have broken both scapulas.
I snapped my right clavicle.

I have broken seven ribs at the front and back over several incidents, and one rib fracture has caused the bone to become misaligned.

I have had my fair share of the ever-so-painful costochondral separation (rib cartilage tears).

I've punctured a lung.

I have broken my jaw.

I fractured my cheekbone.

I have broken my right wrist.

I snapped my left forearm (ulna and radius).

I've broken multiple fingers over the years, including a spiral fracture of my left index finger, breaking my left thumb on three separate occasions, and I have broken three metacarpals in my right hand in one incident.

I have had screws and plates go in and out of my shoulder and arm. I still have titanium in my jaw, right wrist and right hand.

I've had three knee operations, a hernia operation, and surgeries on my arm, wrist, hand and jaw.

The most concerning injury of all is multiple concussions. I estimate that I have been knocked out approximately 25 times. Three of these involve memory loss.

So, yeah, if someone says to me, "You're going to be a cripple when you're older", it is a well-founded comment.

But I'm not.

On 17 May 2023, I wrote on my public blog:

At the present day, I'm currently dealing with significant body alignment issues:

— I've had plantar fasciitis in my left foot since January 2022.

— I have a pain-causing bunion on my left big toe that is about five years old.

— I have yet to be diagnosed, but I believe I have a terrible case of peroneal tendonitis in my left leg.
— My knees (mainly at the patella) cause me significant discomfort with exercise.
— My left knee accumulates and holds fluid when I ski.
— My right hip protrudes at the back.
— The tightness in my tibialis anterior muscles and tendons, combined with tight quadriceps, prevents me from sitting on my heels while kneeling.
— My left glute aches when seated on a chair or driving.
— The top of my cervical spine protrudes at the base of my skull.
— My right shoulder sits half an inch lower than my left.
— I keep tearing my right bicep when overloading it.
— No matter how well hydrated I am, I often cramp my lower limbs with specific static holds.

Suppose I rate my ability on a scale from 1 to 10 to train for up to six months and compete in a marathon, with 0 being unable to run at all and 10 being 100% capable. I am currently a two.

As of writing this chapter today, I've overcome 93% of that list of "present-day" injuries and am currently at an 8.5 on my training ability. For me to comfortably charge steep and deep mountains in my seventies with my little grandchildren shredding in my powdery wake, a lot has to happen between now and then, and that's why I made a conscious effort to start the healing two years ago, so I can not just move freely in my senior years, but thrive.

As of today, I have two massive running goals that I am dedicated to: one is to run 400 metres in under a minute, and the other is to complete the 100-metre dash in 11.99 seconds. A few years ago, I thought I would never run again.

\*\*\*\*

Where I started was with simple movement. I cut out running and impact training and got stuck into Pilates, stretching and breathwork. If you are injury-free and already run or do aerobic sports, then don't stop. If you are recovering from injuries or do not exercise daily, start moving every day with low-impact training. Start walking, cycling, rowing, using an elliptical trainer, practising yoga, weightlifting or swimming. Find something to get you moving, and move.

Document your movement goals for the next 12 months right now.

Here's a list of physical goals and activities that can help you achieve a healthier lifestyle. These activities vary in intensity and type, so there's something suitable for everyone, regardless of fitness level. You may need goals across several activities to get you moving daily for a year.

- Walking is a low-impact activity suitable for all fitness levels. It can be done almost anywhere and is great for cardiovascular health. **Example goal:** "I want to complete 200 3 km walks in 12 months."
- Running or jogging is a higher-impact activity that improves cardiovascular fitness and burns calories. It's ideal for those looking for a more intense workout. **Example goal:** I will find an online guide to prepare for a half marathon, locate a running event scheduled four months from now, and register for it today.
- Cycling: Whether on a stationary bike or a real one, cycling is excellent for cardiovascular health and leg strength. **Example goal:** I will ride two times a week for 52 weeks, increasing the distance until I can ride 80 kilometres without any issues.
- Swimming is a full-body workout that's easy on the joints and suitable for people of all ages and fitness levels.

**Example goal:** swim three days a week until I can swim five kilometres without a break.

- Yoga is excellent for flexibility, balance and mental health. It can be tailored to suit beginners and advanced practitioners.
  **Example goal:** I will do three yoga sessions a week for 52 weeks.
- Pilates focuses on core strength, flexibility and overall body conditioning. It is suitable for various fitness levels.
  **Example goal:** I want to take 100 Pilates classes this calendar year.
- Dancing is fun and engaging. It can be done solo, in pairs or in groups, and it's a great way to raise your heart rate.
  **Example goal:** I want to join a dance studio and learn the foxtrot by December.
- Hiking: Combines cardiovascular exercise with the benefits of being in nature. It's great for building leg strength and endurance.
  **Example goal:** Book Mount X 12 months from now, and I will walk every day, increasing the length of my walk every month, so I am ready to conquer the quest.
- Strength training: Build muscle using weights, resistance bands or body weight. This can be done at home or in the gym.
  **Example goal:** I will do resistance training every day to do 15 consecutive pull-ups and 50 push-ups by August.
- Team sports: Activities like soccer, basketball or volleyball provide a social and competitive way to stay active.
  **Example goal:** I will join the local mixed touch footy team and compete in this season's competition.
- Tennis or badminton: Excellent for cardiovascular health, agility and hand–eye coordination.
  **Example goal:** I will join the local tennis club in the doubles category with my mate Bill and play the next 12 rounds.

You're getting the idea. Other sports to consider are:

**Rowing:** Provides a full-body workout, improving cardiovascular health and muscle strength.

**Martial arts:** Activities like karate, judo or Taekwondo improve strength, flexibility and mental discipline.

**Jump rope:** A simple but highly effective cardiovascular workout that improves coordination.

**Gardening:** A low-intensity activity that involves various movements and can help with physical strength and flexibility.

**Stair climbing:** This activity is excellent for cardiovascular health and leg strength, whether on a stair machine or real stairs.

**Water aerobics:** Combines the benefits of aerobic exercise with the low-impact environment of water, making it suitable for those with joint issues.

**Golf:** Walking the course and swinging the clubs provide moderate physical activity and social interaction.

**Tai Chi:** A low-impact, slow-motion exercise that improves balance, flexibility and mental focus.

I'm going to circle back to strength training ("weights") and elaborate on this exercise option as it is no longer an activity pigeonholed for muscle men or athletes. Health professionals are increasingly recognising resistance training as one of the most powerful actions you can take for your health. In many cases, it's being seen as the number one priority. This is because it offers wide-ranging and profound benefits across nearly every system of the body. As we age, we naturally lose muscle mass—a condition known as sarcopenia—which can lead to frailty, falls and a decline in independence. Resistance training is the only proven method to preserve and build muscle, which in turn supports joint health, extends mobility, and helps maintain a healthy metabolism.

Beyond building muscle, resistance training has significant metabolic benefits. It improves insulin sensitivity and helps regulate blood sugar, making it a powerful tool for preventing and managing type 2 diabetes, obesity and metabolic syndrome. Since muscle is a metabolically active tissue, having more of it increases the number of calories your body burns, even at rest. Resistance training also improves bone density, which is especially important as we age, helping to prevent osteoporosis and reduce the risk of fractures.

Mental health is another benefit. Studies have shown that resistance training can be as effective as antidepressants for some people. It boosts mood, self-esteem, stress resilience, and even cognitive function. And while cardiovascular health is typically associated with aerobic exercise, resistance training also supports heart health by lowering blood pressure, improving cholesterol levels and reducing resting heart rate.

Additionally, resistance training promotes healthy hormone regulation, increasing beneficial hormones such as testosterone, growth hormone and insulin-like growth factor 1 (IGF-1)—all of which contribute to energy, vitality and improved recovery. It also builds functional strength, improving your ability to perform daily activities and reducing the risk of injury, back pain and falls.

One of the most appealing aspects of resistance training is its time efficiency. A couple of sessions per week can deliver impressive results, making it accessible and sustainable for most people. For all these reasons, health professionals are emphasising resistance training not just as a fitness strategy, but as a central pillar of disease prevention, healthy aging and overall wellbeing. As strength coach Dan John puts it, "The fountain of youth is muscle."

I got back into the gym this year, and it's great to see both sexes, all ages and sizes in there.

Here's what you can do. Select one activity from the list. Write down your goal for the activity and stick to it. Fight all odds to achieve each moving goal. Incorporating these activities (or hundreds of others available to you) into your daily routine to make them a habit will significantly contribute to a healthier lifestyle and increased happiness. The key is to find activities you enjoy so that staying active becomes a pleasant and sustainable habit.

You need to do this. Exercise reverses your biological age. It balances hormones, cleans up damaged proteins, repairs damaged DNA, reduces inflammation, lengthens telomeres and reduces "zombie" cells.

If you don't exercise, then neuron-to-neuron connections will deteriorate. Make your challenges difficult. Keep doing hard things and the neuroplasticity changes will enable you to do more complex things.

\*\*\*\*

Up until Lou got sick, I had never seen her train. She was a very active person, and she skied with me, so she got some form of exercise, but I never saw her run, play a sport, or go to the gym. Her oncologist told her she had to get moving.

My notes from this time detail that exercise helps maintain muscle mass, strength and cardiovascular fitness, which can decline during cancer treatment. Exercise allows patients stay more active and independent. It also mitigates common side effects of cancer treatments, such as fatigue, nausea and pain, and aids in managing weight changes associated with treatment. Additionally, regular physical activity can strengthen the immune system, which is particularly beneficial as cancer treatments compromise immunity.

Exercise releases endorphins that improve mood and reduce feelings of anxiety and depression, which are common during cancer treatment. It also enhances sleep quality, which is often disrupted by the stress and discomfort of cancer and its treatment. Further, staying active can speed up recovery times and improve overall prognosis by enhancing the body's ability to heal and recover. Lou was told that regular exercise may reduce the risk of cancer recurrence by regulating hormones and reducing inflammation.

Once again, alcohol needs to be eliminated for a cancer patient to survive; exercise is a necessity to reduce side effects, make you feel better, help you sleep and reduce metastasis. It sounds pretty damn logical for non-cancer patients to thrive.

****

In the introduction to this book, I said that when my depressive state and emotional turmoil bled into my physical appearance and people were asking questions about my welfare, I knew I had to make a change. I constructed a one-page plan and put the skerricks of effort I had left into crawling my way out of the trench that I emotionally resided in.

The three items on the top of that list were:
1. Move every morning for the next 30 days.
2. By this time next week, tell everyone close to me that I am not feeling very good.
3. Make an appointment today with a professional psychologist.

Getting yourself out of an emotional rut when you feel depressed and unmotivated can be challenging. These big three items, combined with a list of other steps, improved my mood and motivation. I hadn't read any self-help information at my point of despair, but much of my plan was around setting small, manageable goals and establishing a daily routine to mitigate feeling overwhelmed and create a sense of accomplishment. Finding some mindfulness techniques, such as deep breathing (because meditation didn't work for me at this point, I was too acute), to reduce stress and improve my mood. Keeping a journal to write down my thoughts and feelings helped me reflect on my progress. I decided to write and draw to see if some creativity would help. I set limits on my screen time and deleted my social media apps for three months. I also started practising gratitude by focusing on the positive aspects of my life, which we still do as a family at the dinner table today.

The item at the top of my list that significantly contributed to my emotional recovery was "Move every morning for the next 30 days." I didn't feel like doing cardio sessions. I couldn't run because of a foot injury, so I committed to diving in the ocean every morning for a month, combined with some water-style aerobic exercises for the physical part. I threw myself off the end of the pier at the furthest end from the shore, so at the very least, I needed to swim more than 50 metres to return to land. By the end of the swim, my body had adjusted to the cold, so I stayed in and did my exercises. It was August in Sydney, so it wasn't your typical swimming weather, which made it a challenge. The five days I was down in the snow with the kids on our holiday, I stayed committed and jumped into the river.

Starting my day with movement combined with a cold water swim was my rudder for the day. Engaging in a physically challenging activity significantly benefited my mental health at this time. Physical exertion triggers the release of endorphins, often referred to as "feel-good" hormones, which helped me elevate my mood and reduced my emotional pain. Exercise lowered my body's stress hormones, adrenaline and cortisol, helping me manage stress and creating a sense of calm. It helped regulate my sleep patterns (as I was waking at three every morning), which is mandatory for my mental wellbeing. The daily physical activity boosted my overall energy levels, combating fatigue and making me feel more productive. Achieving physical goals, even though it was just a 15-minute swim in the cold wintery ocean, boosted my self-confidence and self-esteem, giving me a sense of accomplishment I could take into the day.

Throwing myself into the cold required concentration and focus, which served as a form of mindfulness. You need to focus on your breath to get through the body shock, and it helped to clear my mind of worries and negative thoughts. Overcoming the physical challenges built my mental resilience and taught me to handle other life stressors more effectively. I have since learnt to incorporate regular physical activity into my routine, which provides structure and a sense of purpose, both crucial for mental health stability. Since this month of everyday swimming, engaging in physical activities has been a powerful tool for maintaining and improving my mental health.

I use my 50by50 goals as carrots for movement. Some of my goals are challenging, so they get me moving daily. The goal is not the priority. Sure, there needs to be an end point, but it's more about the system and process I must create to chase that goal. The habits that need to come into play are understanding the goal, learning about it, reaching a flow state for stillness, becoming comfortable with being uncomfortable, and progressing.

Each goal needs to be enjoyable. Collectively, they might be improbable to achieve in a five or six-year period, but I like the idea of constantly moving—of working through goals, enjoying the process, and rewarding myself.

The activities on my list elicit positive emotions. There is engagement, meaning, control, discipline and accomplishment.

## REMEMBER THIS

My most extensive advice is to commit to registering and entering an event a few months from now. This event needs to get you out of your comfort zone and require you to train to complete it. This commitment will get you moving and motivate you to get started. Sign up for at least one this year. Create a process or an environment to achieve that goal. Drag a friend along and sign up today. Make it challenging. Bite off more than you can chew—and chew like crazy.

CHAPTER 9

# MINDFULNESS: REST YOUR BODY, MIND AND SOUL

*"Do not dwell in the past, do not dream of the future, concentrate the mind on the present moment."*
— *Buddha*

For most of my life I was unfamiliar with the term "mindfulness." However, I have always practised it in specific ways without even being aware I was doing so.

There are many definitions of mindfulness, depending on the context. Generally, it refers to being fully present in the moment, paying attention to one's thoughts, feelings and sensations without judgement or distraction. From a psychological perspective, mindfulness involves achieving a mental state that focuses on the present moment while calmly acknowledging and accepting inner experiences. In Buddhism, mindfulness, or sati, is the cultivation of continuous awareness of thoughts, feelings and the surrounding environment, often used as a tool for meditation and spiritual growth.

In secular contexts, mindfulness is widely used as a practical tool to reduce stress, enhance focus and improve emotional wellbeing, often detached from spiritual or religious practices. In therapeutic settings, such as in cognitive behavioural therapy (CBT), mindfulness is used to help people become more aware of their thoughts and feelings without judgement, which can help with stress reduction and emotional regulation. Neuroscientifically, mindfulness is seen as training the brain to focus attention on the present, leading to cognitive improvements like better memory, attention and emotional control. It is also associated with self-compassion, allowing people to observe their thoughts without over-identifying with them, fostering a kinder relationship with themselves.

Over the years, my mindfulness practice has been heavily centred on participating in sports. The more challenging and, to an extent, riskier the sport, the more cleansing it has been for my mind. This is because in contact sports like rugby or exhilarating sports like skiing or motocross, you don't have an option but to bring all of your focus to the present moment. After all, if you don't, you will get hurt.

Action, contact sports and any competitive sports may not seem like traditional forms of mindfulness, but they share key elements that encourage a mindful state of being. These sports require an intense focus on the present moment. Whether you're tackling in rugby, navigating a ski slope, or controlling a motocross bike at high speeds, your attention must be completely focused on what is happening right now. The unpredictability and split-second decision-making leave no room for distractions, aligning with the core principle of mindfulness—being fully present and aware of the "now."

Additionally, these activities heighten body awareness and coordination. The physical exertion, balance and precision they demand force athletes to tune into their bodies, much like traditional mindful practices that encourage a connection between mind and body. Many athletes also experience a "flow state" during these sports; a mental state of total immersion in the task. In this state, time seems to slow down and mental chatter fades, which is deeply connected to the principles of mindfulness. If you have ever experienced a "flow state", it is a beautiful symphony where time dissolves, distractions vanish, and every action feels like an effortless dance with purpose.

Sports also teach emotional regulation. Things can go wrong quickly in rugby, skiing, motocross or other related sports—a bad tackle, a crash or a fall. The ability to stay calm and respond with clarity under pressure is a skill that develops over time, much like traditional mindfulness, which helps manage stress and emotions. The inherent risk in these activities adds another dimension. When facing a challenge that pushes physical and mental limits, the adrenaline rush often sharpens focus, leading to a heightened sense of aliveness and presence that mirrors the goals of mindfulness.

Finally, the community aspect of sports like rugby, or any team sport, or even in shared experiences like skiing or motocross, can enhance mindfulness through the connection and support of others. This sense of teamwork and bonding grounds us in the present moment, fostering awareness of ourselves and those around us.

After reading about mindfulness and having aha moments about why I have felt the inherent need to engage in sports and physical activities, I have embarked on a strategy to find other ways to achieve mindfulness—new ways that are gentle on my body, focus on the soul, and do not just bring me into the right now because of the intensity or the focus required to compete or not get hurt.

Many activities can help cultivate mindfulness and bring awareness to the present moment. Some new mindfulness activities are working for me with the bike and skis left in the garage.

Breathing is going to get some worthy attention in the following few paragraphs. For me, it has been one of the most effective mindfulness practices because it's always available, instantly anchors me to the present moment, and directly influences my nervous system, offering a fast, natural way to calm my mind and body. There is a saying that breathing is the remote control to the nervous system, which I find extremely accurate.

I do Wim Hof breathing five times a week and feel better every time. The Wim Hof breathing technique involves a series of deep, rhythmic breaths followed by periods of breath retention. The process begins with 30 to 40 deep breaths, inhaling fully through the nose or mouth and exhaling without forcing the air out. After the final breath, you exhale fully and hold your breath until you feel the urge to breathe again. Then, inhale deeply, hold for 10 to 15 seconds, and then exhale. This cycle is repeated several times. The technique is designed to increase oxygen levels in the body, reduce stress and improve focus. Often combined with cold exposure and meditation as part of the Wim Hof Method, the practice is associated with benefits like heightened energy, improved mental clarity, enhanced immune function and an overall greater sense of wellbeing. It also helps the body adapt more effectively to stress.

Box breathing is another straightforward and quick breathing exercise that can fit into your day. I learnt box breathing in a slow flow to yin yoga class, and I do this for a few rounds throughout the day when trying to relax. If you are late for a meeting, stuck in traffic, and can't do anything about it. If the kids are niggling each other and you need to tune out. It's a great distraction when you need a quick brain reset. I also do a couple of rounds when I first hop into bed. Box breathing is a deep breathing technique that involves a structured pattern of inhaling, holding the breath, exhaling, and holding again, each for equal counts, typically four seconds, but I like to go for longer. The process begins with inhaling through the nose for X seconds, holding the breath for X seconds, exhaling slowly through the mouth for another X seconds, and then holding the breath for another X seconds before repeating the cycle (X is the same length of time). This technique slows the heart rate, and focusing on breathing and counting instantly dilutes the issue that happens to be taking up too much space in my head.

Another breathing technique that I am able to use is the double inhale, also known as the physiological sigh. It takes up no time and I have even leaned on this during conversation. It's a simple yet powerful breathing technique that helps quickly calm the nervous system and reduce stress. It involves taking two inhales through the nose—one deep breath followed by a shorter, sharper top-up inhale—and then releasing a long, slow exhale through the mouth. This breathing pattern is something we do naturally during moments of emotional release, such as after crying or when trying to calm down. Physiologically, it works by reinflating collapsed alveoli in the lungs, improving gas exchange and reducing carbon dioxide levels in the blood. The long exhale activates the parasympathetic nervous system, which slows the heart rate and promotes a sense of calm. Research, including insights from neuroscientist Dr Andrew Huberman, has shown that the physiological sigh is one of the most effective ways to regulate stress and bring the body back into balance. It's useful in a variety of situations—before sleep, during moments of overwhelm, prior to public speaking, or as part of your daily mindfulness practice—offering a fast, accessible tool for emotional and physiological regulation.

Reading, learning and practising the importance of getting the essential ingredient, oxygen, into our body has elevated my focus on breathing as I treat it as more than just a symbol of life. I am grateful that I am becoming increasingly aware of my breathing, not just in my mindfulness activities but in life and all of its tasks. I still often catch myself mouth breathing shallowly when concentrating or if I am in discomfort or pain. Awareness of this and correcting my technique is a win for my body, mind and soul.

Breathing is our body's most fundamental and automatic function, yet many overlook its significance. Understanding the mechanics and impact of proper breathing can unlock benefits for our physical and mental health. Breathing is the process by which our bodies take in oxygen and expel carbon dioxide, ensuring our cells have the energy they need to function. This process involves the diaphragm, a dome-shaped muscle beneath the lungs, which contracts and flattens during inhalation to allow the lungs to expand. During exhalation, the diaphragm relaxes, pushing air out of the lungs. Proper diaphragmatic breathing—deep breathing from the belly—maximises oxygen intake and supports optimal lung function.

Breathing acts as a bridge between the body and mind. Conscious control of breath can regulate the autonomic nervous system, shifting it between the sympathetic (fight or flight) and parasympathetic (rest and digest) states. For instance, slow, deep breathing calms the nervous system and reduces anxiety, while shallow, rapid breaths may heighten stress. Practices like yoga and meditation emphasise breathing techniques to harmonise the body and mind, improving focus, relaxation and emotional resilience.

Stress activates the sympathetic nervous system, leading to physiological responses such as increased heart rate and rapid, shallow breathing. Prolonged stress can cause chronic over-activation of this system, contributing to various health problems, including high blood pressure and sleep disturbances. Controlled breathing techniques, such as Wim Hof and box breathing, help counteract stress by activating the parasympathetic nervous system. This reduces cortisol levels, slows the heart rate and fosters a sense of calm.

Nose breathing is often overlooked but provides significant advantages over mouth breathing. The nasal passages filter, humidify and warm the air, making it more suitable for the lungs. Nitric oxide, a molecule produced in the sinuses, is inhaled through the nose and has been shown to improve oxygen uptake and circulation. Also, nose breathing promotes proper tongue posture, which is essential for maintaining oral and dental health. Adopting nose breathing can enhance athletic performance, reduce the risk of respiratory infections, and even improve sleep quality by preventing conditions like sleep apnoea.

Breathing correctly is an essential yet underestimated aspect of overall health. Understanding how breathing works, its connection to the body and mind, and the science behind stress management through breath can lead to profound physical and mental benefits. Incorporating techniques like diaphragmatic and nose breathing into daily life is a simple but powerful way to enhance wellbeing and resilience—start by becoming aware of how you breathe at all times of the day.

Along with breathing, I have continued to explore multiple mindfulness practices centred around slowing down and being present to counterbalance my more active brain-resetting activities.

I incorporate mindful stretching or yoga into my day by paying close attention to the sensations in my body as I move through postures. Most mornings, I pair this with observing the sunrise. This powerful practice helps me connect with my body, calm my mind, and set a positive tone for the day. By focusing on the sensations in my body during each posture, I cultivate mindfulness and enhance my ability to stay present in the moment. Combined with natural experiences like watching the sunrise, this practice becomes even more enriching, adding a layer of tranquillity and connection to nature.

Incorporating mindful stretching or yoga into your daily routine offers numerous benefits. It encourages a deeper awareness of your body, helping you understand its needs, strengths and areas of tension. Focusing on your breath and movements can reduce stress and alleviate anxiety while improving flexibility, joint mobility and overall physical strength. Stretching in the morning enhances mental clarity, allowing you to concentrate better and tackle daily challenges with greater focus. Additionally, regular stretching can boost your energy levels, making it easier to start the day with vitality and promote better sleep quality by helping your nervous system unwind.

When combined with observing the sunrise, this practice deepens your connection to nature, fostering feelings of gratitude and awe that promote emotional wellbeing. Mindful stretching also helps process and release stored emotions, creating a sense of inner balance. Starting your day with such a routine enhances your physical health and nurtures your mental and emotional wellbeing, allowing you to embrace the present moment with peace and harmony.

Body scan meditation is another technique that slowly brings awareness to different body parts and notices tension or relaxation. I add this to my breathing or stretching sessions and sometimes during long breath holds. This technique is a powerful way to cultivate awareness of your physical state and develop a deeper connection to your body. Incorporating body scan meditation into your breathing or stretching sessions can enhance the overall benefits of these practices.

Body scan meditation helps release physical and mental stress by consciously noticing and actively relaxing areas of tension. Pairing this with slow, deep breathing can amplify the calming effects, leaving you more at ease. Focusing on each part of your body increases your awareness of how you physically feel, connecting mind and body. This awareness can also help you identify areas that need more care, such as tight muscles or poor posture. The practice also trains your mind to stay in the present moment as you deliberately shift your attention to each body part. Combined with stretching, it keeps your mind engaged, reducing the likelihood of distractions during your session.

Noticing and addressing tension in specific areas can make your stretching routine more effective. Scanning for tightness and relaxing those areas may achieve more profound, comfortable stretches. Additionally, body scan meditation encourages a non-judgemental awareness of your physical sensations, which can calm the nervous system. Integrating it with breathing exercises can further reduce cortisol levels, helping to combat stress and anxiety. This practice also promotes better sleep, allowing you to wind down and release tension before bed. Adding body scan meditation to your breathing or stretching routine makes your practice more holistic, enhancing your mental and physical wellbeing. It's a versatile technique tailored to suit your needs, whether you're seeking relaxation, stress relief or deeper mindfulness.

Mindful eating encourages slowing down and fully savouring your food's flavours, textures and smells, transforming eating into a richer and more intentional experience. This practice goes beyond simply fuelling your body; it helps you reconnect with your senses, fostering a deeper appreciation for the food you consume. While I am not yet proficient at practising mindful eating, I am increasingly aware of the benefits it brings. I've started transitioning from habitually rushing through my meals to trying to slow down, appreciate, and be present during at least some of them. This slight shift has already opened my eyes to how transformative this habit can be—not just for physical health, but for mental wellbeing too.

By slowing down and being present during meals, mindful eating offers several benefits. It enhances digestion, as eating more slowly gives your body time to properly break down food, reducing discomfort like bloating or indigestion. It also improves portion control by helping you recognise when you're full, which can prevent overeating and support a balanced weight. Beyond physical health, mindful eating heightens the enjoyment of food, turning meals into sensory experiences by allowing you to appreciate flavours, textures and aromas fully. It reduces stress by creating a meditative, calming moment that helps you focus on the present and tune out distractions. Perhaps most importantly, it fosters a stronger mind–body connection, helping you better understand your body's hunger and fullness cues and promoting a healthier relationship with food.

While my journey towards mastering this habit is ongoing, every attempt at mindful eating feels like a step in the right direction. It's a process, and I'm learning to celebrate progress rather than perfection. Each meal offers a new opportunity to practice; even small moments of mindfulness can make a meaningful difference.

Walking meditation involves walking slowly and deliberately, paying attention to each step and the sensations in your body. I do this on the beach or in nature, listening to all the sounds around me, which combines mindful listening, a practice of paying full attention to the sounds around you without judgement, whether it's nature's sounds, music, or a conversation. Walking meditation involves walking slowly and deliberately, paying attention to each step and the sensations in your body. This practice encourages mindfulness by connecting movement with awareness, helping you stay grounded in the present moment. For example, focusing on the rhythm of your steps, the feeling of your feet touching the sand or rocky ground, or the gentle sway of your body as you move can anchor your attention and quiet a busy mind. Walking meditation becomes even more enriching when practised on the beach or in nature as it allows you to immerse yourself in the natural world.

Combining walking meditation with mindful listening can deepen your connection to your surroundings. Conscious listening is paying full attention to the sounds around you without judgement, whether it's the rhythmic crashing of waves, the rustle of leaves in the breeze, birds singing, even heavy machinery or distant conversations. This combination heightens your awareness, promoting a sense of peace and presence.

This practice offers numerous benefits. Walking meditation reduces stress by calming the nervous system, while mindful listening helps shift focus away from intrusive thoughts, promoting relaxation. It improves focus and clarity, training the brain to stay attentive and enhancing productivity in other areas of life. Emotional regulation also improves, as mindful walking and listening teach you to acknowledge thoughts and feelings without judgement, cultivating resilience. Additionally, this practice can boost creativity by freeing the mind, especially when you're immersed in natural surroundings. It promotes physical health by improving circulation, supporting cardiovascular health and gently exercising muscles. It deepens your connection to nature, growing a sense of wonder and appreciation for the world around you. Together, walking meditation and mindful listening form a powerful practice that supports mental, emotional and physical wellbeing while offering a serene way to connect with yourself and the environment.

I have taken this one step further in the last few months and followed the advise of Lawrence van Lingen, a movement specialist known for his work on fascia, biomechanics, and nervous system regulation. He emphasises the powerful benefits of backwards walking (also known as retro walking) as a way to restore natural movement patterns, improve coordination and build physical resilience.

He explains that walking backwards stimulates the brain and nervous system in unique ways by challenging proprioception—the body's sense of position in space—which enhances coordination, balance and neuroplasticity. It also helps rebalance dominant movement patterns that are overused from constant forward motion, such as sitting and walking, by opening up the front of the hips and engaging underused muscles like the glutes and hamstrings. Backward walking strengthens the joints, particularly the knees, by activating the vastus medialis obliquus (VMO), and helps retrain foot positioning and stride mechanics, which is especially beneficial for runners and athletes. Additionally, it boosts circulation and lymphatic flow, supporting recovery and joint health.

Van Lingen also ties backward walking to improved breath and fascial health, encouraging slow, intentional movement to promote body awareness, elastic tension throughout the body (tensegrity), and diaphragmatic breathing. To get started, he recommends walking slowly backward for five to 10 minutes, preferably barefoot or in minimalist shoes, with a focus on posture, smooth movement and breath rather than speed. I have been getting a few funny looks and comments while doing this lately, with people yelling, "What are you trying to do, turn back time?" or "That would be much easier going the other way, mate." The comments and looks put a smile on my face, I'm completely cool with it. If I am out walking anyway and at the same time ticking the mindfulness, biomechanics, coordination and physical resilience boxes all at once, I will give anything a go.

Loving-kindness meditation, also known as Metta, is a mindfulness practice focused on cultivating compassion, love and goodwill towards others. It involves silently repeating phrases such as, "May you be happy, may you be healthy, may you be safe, may you have a prosperous 2026", directing these intentions towards people you love or feel need it. There is no reason you can't do this for various others, including yourself, acquaintances, strangers, and even those with whom you may have conflict. I only practice it with people I care about and feel deserve the attention. By the time you have read this, I will have practised it with people I may feel estranged or disconnected from. While these positive thoughts may not tangibly reach others, the practice has the potential to profoundly impact the practitioner, transforming emotional wellbeing and fostering personal growth. Sometimes it feels like you are passing on good juju, which is a nice grounding and connecting feeling.

One of the primary benefits of Metta meditation is its ability to enhance emotional wellbeing. Replacing negative emotions like anger or resentment with positivity and warmth helps elevate one's mood, reduce stress and create a sense of inner peace. Metta meditation also strengthens relationships by promoting empathy, patience and understanding, improving one's perception of and interaction with others. This practice also boosts self-compassion by helping one combat self-criticism, increase self-acceptance, and develop a more positive self-image.

Metta meditation also promotes mindfulness by anchoring your attention in the present moment. Consciously generating kind thoughts requires focus and training your mind to remain aware and attentive. Over time, this can reduce symptoms of anxiety and depression as it rewires your brain to focus on positive experiences and diminishes the impact of negative thought patterns. Furthermore, the practice cultivates emotional resilience by encouraging you to extend compassion even to those who have hurt you, helping you let go of grudges and foster forgiveness.

Another profound benefit of loving-kindness meditation is the sense of connection it creates. While others may not directly feel your compassionate thoughts, Metta creates a sense of interconnectedness, reminding you of the shared human experience and the universal desire for happiness and peace. This practice transforms how you experience life and encourages a more compassionate and harmonious outlook on the world. Through its simplicity and depth, loving-kindness meditation offers a path to more excellent emotional balance, stronger relationships, and a heightened sense of presence.

Gratitude practice is a powerful and transformative habit that involves intentionally focusing on the positive aspects of life, acknowledging the good, and cultivating a deep sense of appreciation for the people, experiences and circumstances that enrich our lives. Rather than letting fleeting moments of joy pass unnoticed, this practice invites us to pause, reflect, and mindfully recognise all that we have to be thankful for—whether grand or seemingly insignificant. Over time, gratitude shifts from being a fleeting emotion to becoming a state of being, one that nurtures emotional resilience, psychological strength, and even physical vitality.

Research consistently shows that cultivating gratitude can

significantly reduce symptoms of anxiety and depression. When we take the time to focus on what is going well in our lives, we naturally divert attention away from negative thought patterns. This positive shift rewires the brain to notice and amplify uplifting experiences, creating new neural pathways that support a more optimistic and resilient outlook. Gratitude doesn't ignore life's difficulties—it simply gives us a way to hold them alongside the good, making challenges feel more manageable and less overwhelming.

Beyond internal benefits, gratitude enhances our relationships and social wellbeing. Sharing gratitude with others—such as expressing thanks during a family meal or acknowledging a friend's support—deepens our sense of connection. These expressions foster mutual respect, empathy and warmth, strengthening the emotional bonds that hold our relationships together. When families build gratitude into their everyday interactions, they create an atmosphere of kindness, understanding and emotional safety, which is especially important for children as they form their values and worldview.

Grateful people also tend to experience a range of physical benefits. Studies have linked regular gratitude practice with lower stress levels, improved sleep quality and stronger immune function. These health advantages contribute to a more balanced and sustainable lifestyle. Because gratitude naturally draws our attention to the present moment, it acts as a form of mindfulness. It grounds us in the now, allowing us to find joy in small, often overlooked moments—like a warm cup of tea, a kind smile, or a moment of silence in a busy day.

Incorporating gratitude into daily routines can be simple yet deeply impactful. For instance, sharing what you're thankful for around the dinner table is an excellent way to foster meaningful family conversations. It provides an opportunity for everyone—adults and children alike—to reflect on the positive moments in their day, no matter how small. These conversations not only build emotional intelligence and empathy in children but also strengthen the collective spirit of the family unit.

When time is limited, keeping a gratitude journal offers a quick and accessible way to engage in the practice. Writing down just three things you're grateful for each day can reinforce positive memories and create a reservoir of encouraging reflections to revisit in more difficult times. Over time, these brief moments of recognition accumulate and help establish a more positive and appreciative mindset.

Gratitude doesn't require grand gestures. It can be built into life's quiet moments—pausing to watch the sunset, taking a deep breath of fresh air, or silently appreciating someone's kindness. These small acknowledgements help embed gratitude into your everyday consciousness, making it not just something you do, but a way of seeing the world.

By committing to a regular gratitude practice, you transform it from an occasional exercise into a consistent, integrated mindset. This shift opens the door to experiencing the full spectrum of its benefits: greater resilience in adversity, stronger relationships, improved wellbeing and a more joyful engagement with life. As you embed gratitude into your routine—through reflection, conversation, or mindfulness—you plant seeds of positivity that ripple outward, enriching not only your own life but the lives of those around you.

Progressive muscle relaxation (PMR) is a therapeutic technique that systematically tenses and relaxes each muscle group in the body, typically starting from the feet and working upward. This method effectively reduces stress, relieves tension and enhances body awareness. By focusing on the contrasting sensations of tension and release, PMR allows us to recognise how stress manifests physically, and consciously alleviate it. PMR offers several specific benefits when applied to areas of strain or injury, which is when I use the practice.

One significant advantage is pain management. PMR can target strained or injured areas to reduce pain perception by improving blood flow, alleviating stiffness and calming inflamed tissues. This process also reduces the guarding reflex, where surrounding muscles tighten to protect the injury but may inadvertently exacerbate discomfort. I have been doing this after a shoulder subluxation (partial dislocation of the shoulder joint), and it has accelerated my recovery. Additionally, PMR fosters a stronger mind–body connection and greater awareness of how the body responds to tension and relaxation. This heightened awareness can help us detect early signs of overuse or re-injury. I also regularly do this for some old foot and leg injuries.

Stress reduction is another key benefit of PMR, particularly for people like me who are dealing with regular strain or injury. Stress usually leads to muscle tension, which can further hinder recovery. Inducing deep relaxation, PMR calms the nervous system, lowers cortisol levels and breaks the cycle of stress-related tension. The technique enhances circulation by stimulating blood flow to targeted areas, delivering oxygen and nutrients essential for tissue repair, and removing metabolic waste that may accumulate in strained or injured muscles.

PMR is a safe and accessible practice that can be done anywhere without special equipment, making it an excellent complement to physical therapy or other recovery treatments. To effectively target specific areas, start by tensing the muscles in the injured or strained region for five to 10 seconds, then slowly releasing the tension and focusing on the sensation of relaxation for 10 to 20 seconds. This process can be repeated as necessary, taking care not to overwork the area. By incorporating PMR into a daily routine, you can enhance recovery, reduce discomfort, and feel a deep sense of relaxation and wellbeing.

While I touched on gratitude journalling, mindful journalling is a powerful tool for self-awareness and personal growth. It provides a safe space to reflect on your thoughts and feelings without judgement, helping you develop greater clarity and emotional resilience. Putting pen to paper (or fingers to keyboard) creates a moment of stillness in a busy day, allowing you to process your experiences and connect with your inner self. Journalling regularly—even if not daily—offers numerous benefits. Reviewing your day through journalling allows you to pause, evaluate, and acknowledge your triumphs and challenges.

Writing about your feelings can reduce stress and anxiety by helping you untangle complex emotions, offering a cathartic way to release negative energy. It also encourages self-compassion and a non-judgemental attitude that allows you to embrace imperfections and celebrate progress rather than focusing on setbacks. Additionally, journalling can improve problem-solving by helping you uncover insights or patterns that will guide better decision-making in the future. It strengthens gratitude by drawing attention to small joys and moments of appreciation that might be overlooked, boosting positivity.

Mindful journalling promotes personal growth by enabling you to track your progress over time, set meaningful goals, and recognise how far you've come. Reviewing your day through journalling can also help you feel grounded, bringing you into the present moment and growing a sense of calm and focus. While aiming to journal daily is admirable, it's important to remember that missing a day isn't a failure; it's part of life's natural ebb and flow. What matters most is returning to the practice when you can, knowing that even occasional journalling contributes to your overall wellbeing. Incorporating this habit into your routine nurtures your mental and emotional health while creating a meaningful practice that enriches your life. I miss more days of journalling when I am in a better head space, which I am okay with, as when times are bumpy, journalling helps me look within. The goal is still to be as regular as I can.

Even seemingly mundane activities, such as showering, can be transformed into powerful mindfulness practices. By focusing on the sensation of warm water cascading over your skin, the gentle rhythm of droplets hitting the tiles, and the soothing scent of soap or shampoo, you can anchor yourself in the present moment. This practice is more than just a way to pass the time—it's a way to nurture your mental wellbeing.

This approach is constructive in grounding my mind. When I bring my full attention to the now, the chatter of my thoughts quietens, and I feel a sense of calm wash over me, much like the water. This simple act helps me shift away from worries about the future or ruminations about the past, allowing my mind to rest and reset.

The benefits of this mindful showering ritual can reduce stress, improve mental clarity, and create a sense of gratitude for the small, everyday moments we often overlook. Over time, integrating mindfulness into daily routines like this can enhance emotional resilience and bring a deeper connection to your body and surroundings. So, the next time you step into the shower, try slowing down and savouring the experience. It's a small but meaningful way to practice self-care and bring a sense of peace into your day.

Finally, mindful conversations involve being fully present while talking to someone, listening without preparing your response or interrupting, and focusing on the other person's words and emotions. Everyone knows someone or has a friend who is always interested in your words. They are highly present in the conversation. They make good eye contact, and they are genuinely listening. There is no reason why you and I can't be that person.

Mindful conversations are a cornerstone of building meaningful connections and mutual understanding in relationships. They involve being fully present while engaging with someone, listening intently without formulating a response or interrupting, and focusing on their words, emotions and underlying needs. Being fully present means setting aside external distractions, like phones or notifications, and internal ones, such as wandering thoughts or preconceptions.

I have formed a habit of lowering my laptop screen and placing my phone face down when I take a phone call, improving my engagement tenfold. This demonstrates respect and attentiveness, creating a space where the other person feels valued. Active listening, a key element, requires giving undivided attention to what is being said, including verbal cues and non-verbal signals like tone, body language and emotions. Reflecting on what you hear, such as by summarising or paraphrasing, shows you truly understand their perspective. Empathy is also vital, as it helps you connect on a deeper level by validating the other person's feelings and making them feel understood. Approaching conversations with an open mind and withholding judgement makes for a safe environment for honest expression.

Practising mindful conversations brings numerous benefits. It improves relationships by nurturing stronger, more authentic connections where people feel appreciated and respected. It also enhances understanding and clarity, reducing misunderstandings and miscommunications by helping you grasp the nuances of someone else's perspective. Mindful conversations support emotional regulation, helping you stay calm and composed even during challenging discussions. Engaging in mindful communication promotes personal growth, cultivating patience, empathy, and self-awareness, which enhance overall communication skills and emotional intelligence.

Your commitment to improving mindful conversations over time is commendable. Growth in this area comes with regular practice, self-reflection and a willingness to adapt. Strategies to support this journey include pausing before responding to absorb what the other person has said, asking open-ended questions to encourage sharing, and reflecting on how mindful you were after each conversation.

I have a long way to go to be a master of this, but it's a goal of mine, and I am continually working on it.

*****

The activities in this chapter provide diverse ways to integrate mindfulness into my daily life, enhancing my overall wellbeing. Please give them a go, along with any other techniques you have read or heard about.

Don't discount sport as a mindfulness practice. If you're willing and able, get back into a sport you once played. Join the local tennis or squash club or any sport that requires your undivided attention. There is no shortage of when and where you can practice mindfulness as, by my definition and application, it is being consciously aware of your thoughts, emotions, bodily sensations and surroundings, and observing your experiences without judgement or trying to change them. This involves accepting things as they are, whether pleasant or unpleasant. By training your mind to focus on the present moment rather than automatically reacting to thoughts or emotions, mindfulness teaches you to respond more deliberately and thoughtfully.

## REMEMBER THIS

In the gentle embrace of the present moment lies a quiet kind of magic—an oasis untouched by the worries of what was or what might be. To be in the now is to savour the melody of life as it plays, each note clear and vibrant. It's the warmth of sunlight filtering through leaves, a friend's laughter that lingers in the air, or the aroma of coffee curling softly into your senses. When we let go of the heavy baggage of yesterday and resist the temptation to script tomorrow, we discover the freedom to experience today fully. In the moment, time slows, colours brighten, and the simple act of being becomes a profound celebration of life. Mindfulness practices have reduced my stress, helping me manage my reactions to stressful situations. Mindfulness has dramatically alleviated my symptoms of anxiety and depression by fostering a greater sense of emotional balance and wellbeing. By training my mind to stay present, mindfulness has improved my ability to concentrate and pay attention to tasks, increasing my productivity and performance. Mindfulness has helped with increased empathy, compassion and non-judgemental listening, improving communication and strengthening relationships. Through mindfulness, I have developed a deeper understanding of myself, my thinking and behaviour patterns and my values, leading to greater self-awareness and personal growth. I know you can, too.

CHAPTER 10

# BECOME A MORNING PERSON

*"The first hour is the rudder of the day."*
– Henry Ward Beecher

I look in the review mirror and think of all of those late nights combined with excessive drinking. There were so many of them. No wonder I failed to maintain an adequate level of happiness. When alcohol consumption and staying up late are combined, the adverse effects are amplified. Alcohol disrupts sleep patterns, leading to poor-quality rest, while sleep deprivation intensifies the fatigue caused by alcohol. This combination increases stress, impairs cognitive functioning, and places additional strain on vital organs like the liver, heart and brain. Not to mention the strain it places on family and loved ones. I often wonder how I made it through the week.

Waking up tired and hungover feels like emerging from a dense fog that clings to your every thought and movement. Your head pounds like a distant drumbeat, a relentless reminder of last night's reckless abandon. The sunlight filtering through the curtains feels like a personal attack, too bright and harsh for your fragile state. Your mouth is parched, tasting faintly of regret and stale alcohol, and your limbs feel as if they've been replaced with lead. The room tilts slightly as you sit up, a cruel echo of the spinning world you stumbled through hours ago. Memories of the night come back in scattered fragments—laughter, music and questionable decisions—and you're left grappling with the uneasy mix of humour and shame. All you crave is water, greasy food and perhaps a time machine to undo it all, but for now, the day looms ahead, demanding you function despite the chaos in your body and mind. Wow, I am glad those days are more than two years behind me!

Apart from giving up the booze, the start of becoming a morning person is getting the night before sorted. I am going to go one step further because for me, my good night's sleep doesn't begin when my head hits the pillow—it starts with my very first breath when I rise in the morning.

The sun peeks through my skylight, and with the slow blink of waking eyes, the day stretches ahead like a canvas. What I paint on it will echo back to me in the quiet hours of the night.

The way you wake—whether with a sigh or a smile—lays the first brick in the foundation of your next slumber.

You roll out of bed and step into the rhythm of the day. The morning light signals to your circadian clock: It's time to be alert, to move, to live. You sip your tea, not too late, and feel the gears turning in your brain. Movement matters. Maybe it's a walk, a run, or simply standing in the sun, letting your skin drink in the light like a plant turning towards the sun. All these things are whispers to your body: We're awake now. When the time is right, we'll rest.

You eat, ideally with intention. You work, ideally with presence. You breathe, hopefully with awareness. The choices you make from breakfast to bedtime are not just about productivity or nourishment—they're about crafting the conditions for restoration. Each decision is a message to your body: We care about you. You'll be safe to let go later.

Midday passes, and your attention flickers. Your phone pings. The world presses in. But somewhere in the background of your mind, there's a soft reminder: Protect the night. Maybe that means stepping outside again. Perhaps it means letting the stress pass through instead of holding it tightly in your shoulders. Perhaps it means deciding not to open that email at 7.30 pm.

Early to bed and early to rise, right? A good night ritual is essential to becoming a morning person because it lays the foundation for restful sleep and an energised start to the day. The quality of your morning often reflects the preparation you've done the night before. Establishing a consistent bedtime helps regulate your circadian rhythm, making it easier to fall asleep and wake up at the same time each day. Creating a wind-down routine that includes calming activities like reading, meditating, drinking herbal tea, or taking a warm bath or shower signals to your body that it's time to relax. This reduces stress and promotes the production of melatonin, a hormone that aids sleep.

One of the most important habits to adopt is limiting screen time before bed, preventing the disruptive effects of blue light on your circadian rhythm and leading to deeper, more restorative sleep. It's habitual for many of us to stream a TV series before sleeping or to scroll through the news. Dropping this habit has made the times I decide to take a break on the weekend and watch a movie or chip away at a series rewarding; I feel like I have earned this downtime luxury and not abused it.

Ensuring that your sleep environment is quiet, dark and cool also contributes to higher-quality rest, which is vital for waking up feeling refreshed. Preparing for the next day, such as laying out clothes or planning your morning by simply checking the next day's calendar and doing a quick mental run-through of what needs to happen, will reduce decision fatigue and potential morning stress.

A well-rested body and mind will naturally feel more energised and focused, making it easier to stick to a morning routine. Reducing late-night stimulation, such as avoiding caffeine or intense work, helps balance your nervous system, making the transition into sleep smoother. I even refrain from drinking green tea after midday because of its caffeine content. Getting the recommended seven to nine hours of sleep ensures you wake up with the energy and focus you need for a productive morning. I strive to get at least seven hours of sleep each night. According to my Garmin data from the past 24 months, I am just short of this goal, so I need to improve on this. However, my sleep quality is consistently high, and I pick up a little more sleep time over the weekend. The night ritual has been a key component of my improved sleep. Over time, the consistency of an effective night ritual builds momentum, making early mornings more enjoyable and sustainable. My night routine also sets the example for the kids.

Incorporating simple activities like dimming the lights, reflecting on the day, and preparing for the next one can ease the transition to bedtime, promoting a better night's sleep. My process isn't rigidly formal, but as I wind down the kids around 9 pm, I move into relaxing activities. I will read or journal. If I'm too tired for this, I'm already winning, as I know I will be asleep within minutes of my head hitting the pillow.

It's good to reflect on the day. What was good about it? What wasn't pleasant? Did I suffer any imagined troubles? Did I focus only on the things that I can control? Did I choose each situation with the most appropriate perspective? What emotions can I let go of? What am I grateful for? Did I challenge myself today?

A nighttime herbal tea is part of my process and has both mental and physiological benefits. A good tea can be a game changer for restful sleep and overall wellbeing. Blends containing soothing herbs like chamomile, valerian root and lavender are known for their calming properties, helping to reduce stress and anxiety. The warm beverage can signal to your body that it's time to wind down, promoting relaxation and easing you into sleep. Many herbal teas are caffeine-free, making them perfect for late evenings, and their natural antioxidants can support your immune system while you rest. A cup of herbal tea is not just a bedtime ritual; it's a soothing way to nourish your body and mind. I like having my tea not long after dinner as I start to reduce fluid intake so I lessen the need to get up in the night to empty my bladder.

Box breathing is one of the first things I will do when the lights go out. A few rounds takes only a minute, slowing the heart rate and inducing a little reset. If my body is still alert, then listening to a podcast or background music, sounds like the ocean or sound healing bowls, is something that works for me. Ultimately, an effective night ritual goes beyond just sleep preparation—it sets the stage for a successful, energised morning, allowing you to become the morning person you aspire to be. I don't doubt you can cut out a good hour of dead time in your evening. Be the catalyst to re-engineer your household's night routine and break the cycle of late nights and unhealthy habits.

My Garmin sleep data highlights two consistent patterns. First, the timing of exercise has a measurable impact on my sleep quality. When we train earlier in the day, sleep efficiency and recovery metrics improve, whereas late-evening sessions are associated with reduced sleep quality. Given that some of my current group training takes place at night, this remains a limiting factor. Second, late food intake disrupts my sleep. When meals are finished at least two hours before bedtime, sleep quality scores—particularly deep and REM sleep—show substantial improvement.

There is no shortage of studies detailing how sleep is crucial for longevity due to its profound impact on various aspects of physical and mental health. During deep sleep, the body engages in cellular repair and maintenance processes, essential for longevity and overall health. Inadequate sleep is linked to cognitive decline and an increased risk of neurodegenerative diseases, like Alzheimer's. Poor sleep is associated with hypertension, heart disease and stroke.

Sleep plays a role in strengthening the immune system, enhancing the body's ability to defend against infections and diseases.

Long-lasting sleep deprivation can lead to increased inflammation, a factor in various chronic diseases. Sleep helps regulate inflammation levels. Sleep is crucial for maintaining balanced hormone levels, including those that influence appetite, stress response and growth. A quality sleep routine paired with positive coping strategies can make you more resilient against depression and anxiety. Sleep needs to be a priority.

I like getting up early as it makes my day way more productive due to biological, psychological and environmental factors. One key reason is our body's circadian rhythm, which operates on a 24-hour cycle and regulates sleep, energy levels and hormone release. In the morning, cortisol, a hormone associated with alertness, naturally peaks, promoting focus and cognitive sharpness. This contrasts with the late afternoon or evening, when energy levels often dip. I have become a good sleeper, so my brain is well-rested when I wake, leading to better cognitive functioning. This makes my mornings ideal for tasks requiring concentration, creativity and problem-solving. I have been told that sleep also helps consolidate memories. Perhaps this is why I wake up with clearer thinking.

Mornings tend to come with fewer distractions. My environment at home before 6.30 am is dead quiet—the kids are fast asleep, and emails, meetings, or social interactions are nil—allowing for better focus on whatever task I choose. I also don't look at my phone for the first two hours of the day.

Like a muscle, willpower is also at its peak in the morning. After rest, my decision-making abilities and self-control are more robust, whereas decision fatigue can often set in as the day progresses, making it harder to stay productive. For the most part, I also have a structured morning routine involving exercise (usually stretching and an ocean dip) and/or mindfulness, which further primes my brain for a more efficient day.

Psychologically, the morning often brings me a sense of optimism—a fresh start—that boosts my motivation. By nightfall, the accumulation of slight or high stress from the day leads to mental fatigue and lower productivity. Not much productivity happens in my household after 7 pm for any of its three occupants, so it's in our interest to wind up the day calmly and efficiently.

It's not always smooth sailing, as sleep is directly tied to my emotions. It's harder for me to get up early when I feel flat and am not on top of my feelings, because my low energy and mood can sap my motivation and make the effort of starting the day feel overwhelming. When my feelings are out of balance, I'm susceptible to falling into negative thinking patterns or feeling mentally drained, making bouncing out of bed and facing the day seem daunting. In these moments, my brain gravitates towards comfort and avoidance, making it tempting to hit the snooze button or get up and move without purpose. This emotional flatness makes even small tasks seem like significant hurdles, leading to a lack of drive that disrupts my usual morning productivity.

\*\*\*\*

I started to slip on my early rising habit in mid-2024. Part of my mini plan to get back on top was to watch the sunrise for 10 consecutive days and incorporate Dr Huberman's advice to look at the morning sunlight. It took three days to take effect, and I have been waking up before my alarm since, even through emotional dips that require effort to stay disciplined.

Dr Andrew Huberman, a neuroscientist and professor at Stanford University, promotes a morning technique involving exposure to natural sunlight, preferably within the first hour of waking. This practice is grounded in neuroscience, as our circadian biology is designed to regulate the body's internal clock. When you expose your eyes to sunlight in the morning, it activates special receptors in the eyes called melanopsin, which contain retinal ganglion cells that are particularly sensitive to the blue light found in natural sunlight. These cells send signals to the brain's master clock, the suprachiasmatic nucleus (SCN) in the hypothalamus, responsible for regulating the sleep–wake cycle and other physiological processes.

Exposure to morning sunlight helps suppress the release of melatonin, a hormone that induces sleep, making you feel more awake and alert. It also reinforces the timing for melatonin production later in the evening, promoting better sleep when it's time to wrap up the day. Sunlight exposure enhances the body's natural cortisol pulse in the morning, to kick you to get after it. It boosts mood by increasing levels of serotonin, a neurotransmitter linked to improved mood, focus and calmness. Aligning your body with the natural light–dark cycle also supports metabolism, helping regulate the glucose processes and appetite control.

To apply this technique, Dr Huberman says it's best to get outside within 30 to 60 minutes of waking up and spend 10 to 30 minutes in the sunlight, depending on the day's brightness. Outdoor light is much more effective than indoor light, even on cloudy days, so going outside when you wake up should be engineered into your day. Avoid wearing sunglasses or looking through windows, as these can reduce the amount of sunlight reaching your eyes.

I start my stretching routine at Balmoral Beach just before sunrise. While stretching, I gaze at the sun between different stretch holds while breathing into the part of my body that I am stretching. I also look at the sun when I am in the water. I can look directly into the sun with zero discomfort in my eyes when it first hits the horizon. If the sun has been in the sky for a little while, I choose not to stare directly at it. Andrew Huberman's popular light and sun exposure guide works. This simple practice has optimised my wakefulness, mood and energy throughout the day while punching out better sleep at night. I have been an early riser since becoming a father as I have to accomplish many things during the day, but Huberman's process makes the practice natural and easy.

In addition to regulating circadian rhythms, exposure to morning sunlight is essential for maintaining healthy levels of vitamin D, synthesised in the skin in response to sunlight. Adequate vitamin D levels are necessary for bone health, immune function and mood regulation.

If you struggle to get up, commit to doing the first five days in a row with a friend so you don't let each other down. Do some exercise and get morning light exposure together. It will get easy very fast.

\*\*\*\*

There's a quiet magic in waking up early when the world is still wrapped in the soft glow of dawn. The air feels fresher, the sky is brushed with pastel hues that slowly melt into gold as the sun rises. It's a time when everything feels possible, like the day ahead is a blank canvas waiting for my touch. The stillness offers a moment of reflection, a gentle pause before the day's demands rush in. Birds sing their first songs and the light dances through trees, casting long shadows that stretch across the earth. In these moments, the world feels new, and a peaceful clarity makes even the simplest tasks seem infused with purpose and grace.

Get some exercise first thing in the morning, whether it's light or strenuous. A walk, a dip in the ocean, a stretching session, a group gym class; anything.

Another ingredient to add to the mix is setting your intention for the day. There is a quote from Marcus Aurelius that I like:

*When you wake up in the morning, tell yourself: the people I deal with today will be meddling, ungrateful, arrogant, dishonest, jealous and surly. They are like this because they can't tell good from evil. But I have seen the beauty of good, and the ugliness of evil, and have recognised that the wrongdoer has a nature related to my own - not of the same blood and birth, but the same mind, and possessing a share of the divine. And so none of them can hurt me. No one can implicate me in ugliness. Nor can I feel angry at my relative, or hate him. We were born to work together like feet, hands and eyes, like the two rows of teeth, upper and lower. To obstruct each other is unnatural. To feel anger at someone, to turn your back on him: these are unnatural.*

Now, Marcus was the Roman emperor, so his day would be nothing like mine, but I still deal with people, and people are complex. In early 2024, I created my version of this quote. I added some daily reminders, objectives and intentions.

My daily intention changes over time based on what needs more focus. At the time of writing this chapter, each morning before reviewing and updating my to-do list, I read:

People today will attempt to disrupt my equanimity. Create space between every stimulus and my emotional 'reaction' and 'respond' with Virtue. In every situation, choose the handle with the most appropriate perspective. Focus on what I can control. Don't suffer imagined troubles. Ask myself at every decision point, is this essential?

Arete!

My purpose is to be the best version of myself, nurture my children, set an example they not only respect but emulate, give them all the love and attention they need, radiate calmness and positive energy that's felt by those around me, and authentically influence others. Hence, they become better versions of themselves. I believe in the power of love, support and understanding, and I aim to create a warm, caring environment where those around me can flourish—showing compassion, empathy and generosity, spreading love and kindness in everything I do. To inspire and educate others, helping them discover their passions and achieve their full potential. I strive to be a positive influence and a source of knowledge, always encouraging growth and lifelong learning. I am committed to pursuing personal growth and happiness. To continually challenge myself, explore new interests, and cultivate a life filled with joy, fulfilment and balance.

My priority is to have what is essential and, second, have what is enough. Essentials include feeding my children healthy food, clothing them, providing them with warm, comfortable shelter and every opportunity in education and co-curricular activities. It is affording the time to be present in their lives. Having enough is holidaying as a family once a year and continuing to live a balanced life where work and play are equal. If I live a life of virtue, my success and happiness will ensue.

Eudaimonia!

Today, I will:
— Observe my mind and exercise cognitive distancing
— Be disciplined
— Have no ego
— Stay calm with the kids. No raised voice
— *Hara hachi bu* (eat until you're 80% full)

- No sugar
- Eat quality meat
- Prepare more food
- Vegetables and fruit – eat the rainbow
- Green & jasmine tea, hydrate
- No cow's milk and minimal diary
- Bring movement and breath together – for presence and consciousness
- Be present in my interactions with everyone
- Rush less
- Be friendly to strangers
- Smile
- Be more social
- Spend more time with friends and family
- More time in nature
- Progress the business
- Pursue my passions!
- 50by50 – Run, ride, row, surf, handstand, resistance training and wheelies!

Reading this list each morning reminds me what I want to focus on, laying a positive foundation to set my feet in a positive direction until it's time to wind up the day, put it up for review and reflect on how I did.

## REMEMBER THIS

A good night's rest begins with your very first conscious breath.

Every action and reaction throughout your day shapes the quality of your sleep. It's not random—it's a cycle, and it thrives on awareness.

So when the day winds down and you finally lie back, it's not a collapse. It's a return. A full-circle homecoming.

Your body—well moved.

Your mind—well used.

Your heart—maybe even light.

Sleep doesn't just show up. It responds to your invitation. And that invitation is written in every choice you made from the moment you opened your eyes.

Own your morning. Shape your night. Go after it.

CHAPTER 11

# POST-TRAUMATIC GROWTH: RISE AND RISE AGAIN

*"Sometimes, when you're in a dark place, you think you've been buried, but you've been planted."*
– Christine Caine

I am not sure if anyone escapes having to deal with trauma. Trauma can result from a wide range of experiences, and what impacts one person profoundly might not affect another in the same way. Common causes of trauma include abuse, whether physical, emotional, verbal or sexual, as well as the loss of a loved one through death or separation. Natural disasters like earthquakes, hurricanes and floods can also leave lasting emotional scars, as can car or other severe accidents. Bullying or harassment—whether at school, in the workplace or online—can have a profound effect, as can witnessing violence in any form, including domestic, community or mass violence.

Childhood neglect or abandonment is a significant source of trauma, along with medical trauma caused by severe illness, surgery or prolonged hospitalisation. Experiencing war or conflict, as either a civilian or a combatant, is another deeply traumatic experience, as is sexual assault or harassment. Racism and discrimination, whether experienced or witnessed, can also cause lasting emotional harm. Sudden financial instability, such as the loss of a job or the breakdown of a significant relationship, as in a divorce, can be highly traumatic. Being falsely accused of a crime or wrongdoing, dealing with substance abuse or addiction in the family, or experiencing homelessness or severe poverty can leave lasting scars. Betrayal by someone you deeply trust, adoption or separation from biological parents, and involvement in the justice system, including incarceration, can also be sources of trauma.

Chronic exposure to toxic environments such as unsafe neighbourhoods, dysfunctional families or hostile workplaces can significantly impact mental health. The list goes on, and the effects can be devastating.

\*\*\*\*

My relationship with Lou wasn't perfect, but it was solid. As the years passed, we understood each other better and became more accommodating. Kids improved our lives instead of making them more challenging. We were aligned on most things. We loved each other. We never doubted getting old together.

Losing Lou so quickly to cancer was traumatic. Knowing I had to parent on my own with no preparation was traumatic. Having to keep a business alive while grieving was traumatic. When Lou passed, my world shattered utterly. The grief was overwhelming— emotional, physical and spiritual. I felt like I was drowning in the weight of her absence, unsure how to move forward. But as I looked into the eyes of Noah and Evie, the children Lou had gifted me, I realised I couldn't let the loss consume me. They needed me, and I needed them. They became the anchor that kept me grounded and the driving force behind my transformation. Slowly but surely, I began to grow in ways I could never have imagined.

"A happy life consists not in the absence, but in the mastery of hardships," writes Helen Keller. She also said, "Character cannot be developed in ease and quiet. Only through experience of trial and suffering can the soul be strengthened, ambition inspired, and success achieved."

When I lost Lou, it felt like time stood still. I was consumed by grief, and the life we had built together seemed impossibly far away. Yet every time I observed or even thought about our kids, I knew I had a choice to make. I could stay buried in despair, or I could find a way to honour her memory by being the parent she would have wanted me to be. That realisation became my turning point. It wasn't, and still isn't, an easy journey and it certainly wasn't linear. Some days felt heavier than others. But through the pain, I found strength in my love for my children and my determination to build a meaningful life for them and myself.

My kids taught me to appreciate life's preciousness even amid loss. Their laughter, curiosity and resilience reminded me of the beauty in small, everyday moments—the sun's warmth, the joy of a quiet morning and the comfort of a hug. They inspired me to find strength I didn't know I had. There were challenges I doubted I could face without Louise, but I did because I had to. Each small victory— preparing their lunch, helping with homework, celebrating a milestone, or simply being present for them, which was 24/7 in the first three years—reminded me of my capacity to endure and adapt.

The experience also opened my heart in unexpected ways. I deepened my relationships with the people around me, both for myself and for my kids. I reconnected with family, leaned on friends, and forged new bonds that provided support and love when we needed it most. Vulnerability became a source of strength, not weakness. Through it all, I found ways to honour her memory—by raising our children with our shared values, pursuing passions I had once set aside, and living a life I know she'd be proud of. My kids were the greatest motivators for this growth. I wanted them to see that it's possible to find hope and meaning even in the face of profound loss.

Today, I can say that I am not just surviving—I am thriving. The pain of losing my wife will always be a part of me, but it no longer defines me. Instead, it fuels my drive to live fully and meaningfully. I've learnt to carry her love and endless energy forward, letting it inspire my actions and guide my journey. This experience has shown me that even in the depths of grief, there is room for growth. Healing isn't about forgetting; it's about transforming the pain into something meaningful. With my kids by my side, I've emerged stronger, more connected, and deeply grateful for the lessons we've learnt together.

\*\*\*\*

Post-traumatic growth (PTG) is a psychological concept that describes positive psychological change experienced as a result of struggling with highly challenging life circumstances. It is the antithesis of post-traumatic stress disorder (PTSD), highlighting the potential for people to emerge from trauma with a greater appreciation for life, improved relationships, a sense of increased personal strength, a recognition of new possibilities and spiritual development. Unlike the negative consequences often associated with trauma, PTG focuses on the transformative power of such experiences.

The term "post-traumatic growth" was coined by psychologists Richard Tedeschi and Lawrence Calhoun in the mid-1990s. Their research showed that people who experience trauma often report significant personal growth in the aftermath. PTG is not merely a return to baseline functioning, but rather an improvement in one's psychological functioning beyond the pre-trauma level. This growth is not universal; not everyone who experiences trauma will undergo PTG, and it is essential to recognise that the absence of PTG does not imply a lack of resilience or coping.

PTG manifests in several key areas. Trauma can lead us to develop a renewed sense of gratitude for life and its everyday moments. Survivors often express a deeper appreciation for the small pleasures and are more mindful of the present. Traumatic experiences can strengthen interpersonal relationships. Survivors may feel more compassion and empathy for others, leading to more substantial and more meaningful connections. Many people discover an inner strength they were unaware of. Overcoming adversity can build confidence and self-efficacy as survivors recognise their resilience and ability to navigate future challenges. Trauma can open up new opportunities and directions in life. People might pursue different career paths, hobbies or life goals they had not considered before. For some, trauma prompts a spiritual or existential awakening. This can involve deepening religious faith or a broader connection to humanity and the universe.

Fostering PTG involves both personal effort and support from others. Encouraging people to process their trauma cognitively can aid in PTG. This consists of making sense of the traumatic event, reinterpreting its meaning, and integrating it into one's life narrative. Therapy, journalling and reflective practices can facilitate this process. Having a strong support system is crucial. Friends, family and support groups provide emotional support, validation and a sense of belonging. Sharing one's experiences and hearing others' stories can be profoundly healing. Engaging with mental health professionals such as psychologists, counsellors or therapists can be beneficial.

When I hit my lowest point, I engaged with a therapist to help me off the floor. I only needed to see them four times, but it was an ingredient in feeling and acting better. It was a sanctuary where I could unravel the chaos within. It offered me a safe space to confront buried emotions and speak truths I hadn't yet voiced. Through the guidance of a compassionate therapist, I learnt to understand my pain, reframe negative thoughts, and build on my sense of self-worth. I needed a guided step out of a shadowed labyrinth, bringing more clarity, strength and hope. In the book *The Boy, the Mole, the Fox and the Horse* by Charlie Mackesy, the horse says, "Asking for help isn't giving up. It's refusing to give up", which is so true but often not embraced.

Learning to view the trauma through a positive lens can be transformative. This does not mean denying the pain, but recognising the potential for growth and positive change that can arise from the experience. Practices that promote mindfulness and meditation can help you stay grounded and focused on the present moment. These practices can reduce stress and anxiety, allowing you to approach your trauma with a calmer, more centred mindset. Pursuing activities that bring joy and a sense of purpose can aid recovery. Whether volunteering, engaging in creative pursuits, or taking up new hobbies, these activities can provide a sense of accomplishment and fulfilment. Physical wellbeing is closely linked to mental health and can provide the energy and resilience needed to navigate recovery from trauma.

Emotional regulation is another vital component in fostering PTG. Knowing that we can change our physiological state through deep breathing, progressive muscle relaxation and biofeedback can be empowering. These techniques help regulate the body's stress response, reducing the physical symptoms of anxiety and trauma. When people learn to manage their emotional responses, they can approach their experiences with a clearer mind and a more balanced emotional state, making it easier to process trauma and integrate it into their lives in a positive way.

Disclosure, or acknowledging and openly sharing what has happened, is also crucial in PTG. By openly discussing their experiences, people can begin to process and make sense of their trauma. This acknowledgment helps validate their feelings and experiences, reducing the burden of carrying the trauma alone.

I find that talking about my emotions out loud to someone while detailing the situation is a massive help. Sharing one's story with trusted people can provide relief and promote healing, as it allows for emotional release and connection with others who offer support and understanding. Acceptance of the reality of the trauma and recognising it for what it is can also lead to a sense of closure and peace, enabling you to move forward with your life.

Acceptance is a powerful step in PTG. Accepting what has happened, without denial or suppression, allows you to constructively integrate your experiences into your life narrative. Acceptance does not mean approval of the trauma but acknowledging its occurrence and impact. This acknowledgment can reduce internal conflict and free up emotional energy, which can be directed towards growth and healing. Additionally, breaking neurophysiological loops—patterns of thought and behaviour that reinforce negative emotions and stress responses—is essential. Trauma can create these loops, where the brain continually replays distressing memories, leading to prolonged emotional suffering. Techniques such as cognitive restructuring, mindfulness and neurofeedback can help interrupt these patterns, enabling the brain to form new, healthier pathways. By breaking these loops, you can reduce the intensity of traumatic memories and decrease their impact on daily life, paving the way for positive transformation.

Post-traumatic growth highlights the potential for positive transformation following trauma. It is testament to the resilience and adaptability of the human spirit. By understanding the concept of PTG and implementing strategies to foster it, people can emerge from their traumatic experiences as survivors and as people who have grown and thrived despite adversity. This growth journey requires time, support and self-compassion, but it offers a powerful narrative of hope and resilience.

\*\*\*\*

After my long stretch of feeling so good after breaking down, when I looked in the revision mirror, there was a mosaic of both physical and mental health ingredients that got me back on track, such as healthy relationships, better sleep, balanced work, exercise and movement, mindfulness, increasing healthy habits, mindset, diet and nutrition and shutting the door on alcohol.

I believe you can make a choice about which path you will take when dealing with trauma; I think you can use the power of your mind to take a PTG route. I often quote one of Marcus Aurelius' famous sayings: "The impediment to action advances action. What stands in the way becomes the way." This quote, attributed to the Roman Stoic philosopher in his *Meditations*, conveys a core Stoic principle: challenges and obstacles are not just hindrances but opportunities for growth, learning, and progress. Instead of seeing obstacles as reasons to stop, they can be viewed as necessary experiences that push us to find creative solutions and become stronger. We learn to adapt, refine our skills, and build resilience by facing difficulties head-on.

The key lies in shifting our mindset to embrace challenges as part of life's natural flow—understanding that resistance and hardship don't block the path; they *are* the path. This process helps us move closer to our goal and equips us with valuable knowledge and experience. In essence, the quote reminds us to reframe how we perceive challenges, recognising that what seems like a setback, as devastating and traumatic as some can be, can often be the very thing that leads us to a better place than before our grief or setback took hold of us.

This approach can be transformative in dealing with trauma because it shifts the focus from viewing painful experiences as purely destructive to seeing them as opportunities for growth and healing. Trauma often feels like an insurmountable obstacle, but adopting the mindset expressed in the quote encourages us to face it directly and work through it, allowing us to find meaning and resilience. By confronting trauma instead of avoiding it, we can start to process the pain, understand its impact and learn from it. This approach helps us recognise that the experience, while challenging, can teach us valuable lessons about ourselves—such as our capacity for endurance, the importance of self-compassion, and the strength we possess to rebuild. The obstacle (trauma) becomes the way forward by guiding us towards growth through therapy, building supportive relationships or finding a new purpose. Ultimately, this mindset allows us to reframe trauma not as something that permanently defines us or limits our potential, but as a pivotal moment that can lead us to a deeper understanding of life, greater empathy for others and a stronger sense of self. We can transform pain into progress and hardship into healing by embracing the challenge.

****

I have focused on the word "trauma" in this chapter. I need to be mindful that it doesn't have to be an event or a series of events that can take you down. Unhappiness can sometimes feel like it happens for no reason, even when there is no apparent external trigger. Emotional turmoil isn't always tied to specific events or circumstances. One possible cause is chemical imbalances in the brain. The brain relies on a delicate balance of chemicals like serotonin, dopamine and norepinephrine. When this balance is disrupted due to genetics, stress, or other factors, it can lead to feelings of sadness, hopelessness or lack of energy, even without an apparent cause. Additionally, feeling flat or depressed can be hereditary, meaning it may run in families, and those with a genetic predisposition may experience unhappiness without any external stressors or adverse life events.

Chronic stress or burnout can build up gradually, leading to mental health struggles. Hormonal changes, especially during puberty, pregnancy, postpartum and at menopause, or issues like thyroid problems, can also contribute to feelings of unhappiness. Seasonal affective disorder (SAD), for example, is a type of depression linked to certain times of the year, typically in winter, due to lack of sunlight or shorter days.

Unresolved emotional trauma can also resurface and manifest as unhappiness, even if you're not consciously aware of the connection. Chronic health conditions or illnesses can lead to feeling your worst, and sometimes their mental health impacts are overlooked. A lack of purpose or fulfilment can also contribute to negative feelings that are hard to overcome, especially when life starts to feel monotonous or empty. Similarly, continuous exposure to negative news, comparisons on social media, or overstimulation can gradually lead to feelings of inadequacy or hopelessness.

Lastly, sometimes a breakdown or emotional chaos occurs due to unknown factors, as the mind is incredibly complex. It combines biology, psychology and external circumstances that can interact uniquely in each individual.

When you find yourself in an emotional rut—whether it's caused by trauma, stress, or other challenges—it's common to feel overwhelmed by self-blame. You might criticise yourself for not handling the situation "better" or for "breaking down", as though emotional struggles signify a personal failure. This mindset often stems from societal pressures to always appear strong, resilient and in control. However, it's essential to understand that emotional breakdowns are not signs of weakness, but natural responses to overwhelming circumstances. Just as your body reacts to physical injury with pain or fatigue, your mind reacts to emotional strain with feelings of despair, confusion or exhaustion. These responses are signals that something needs attention and care.

Blaming yourself in these moments only deepens the emotional rut. It creates a cycle of guilt and self-criticism that prevents healing and growth. Instead of seeing breakdowns as failures, they can be reframed as a call to pause, reflect, and prioritise your wellbeing. They provide an opportunity to understand your limits, build resilience and develop self-compassion. Recognising that everyone faces emotional challenges at some point can also help alleviate the pressure of perfection. You are not alone in your struggles. Seeking help or giving yourself grace is an act of courage, not defeat. By shifting your perspective, you can see emotional ruts as temporary and manageable rather than as insurmountable obstacles.

Seneca, the Stoic philosopher, often emphasised the importance of cultivating a healthy relationship with oneself. When he speaks of "being a friend to yourself", he encourages self-compassion, self-awareness and inner peace. To be a friend to yourself means treating yourself with kindness and understanding rather than harsh criticism or judgement. Just as you would forgive a friend's faults, Seneca advises that you should also forgive your own and focus on growth instead of dwelling on mistakes. He believed in the importance of self-awareness and regular reflection to better understand your thoughts, emotions and actions. Doing this allows you to align your decisions with your values and virtues, acting in your best interests, much like a true friend would guide you.

Moreover, being a friend to yourself involves maintaining inner peace and creating a tranquil space free from unnecessary worries or the pressures of external validation. Seneca suggests finding contentment in simplicity, reducing desires and focusing on what truly matters. A friend also advocates for you, helping you make choices that support your wellbeing. Similarly, Seneca encourages you to prioritise your long-term good over fleeting pleasures or harmful distractions. Practically, being a friend to yourself involves practising self-care, nurturing your physical and mental health, and reflecting on your actions to ensure they align with your values. It also means forgiving past mistakes and focusing on moving forward rather than comparing yourself to others. Ultimately, Seneca's advice is about self-respect and balance. By being your friend, you become a source of strength and wisdom for yourself, enabling you to live a life honouring your higher self.

## REMEMBER THIS

As humans, we need to remember that trauma and unhappiness are inevitable parts of life, arising from various sources like abuse, loss, accidents, bullying, medical conditions, and even emotional struggles like grief or stress. While it can devastate, trauma also presents the possibility for growth.

Positive psychological changes, such as increased personal strength, improved relationships, and a renewed sense of life's meaning, arise from confronting adversity. It involves understanding and accepting the trauma and transforming it into an opportunity for self-improvement and deeper connections. Therapy, mindfulness, supportive relationships, and reframing the trauma positively are key to fostering post-traumatic growth.

While trauma may leave lasting emotional marks, it does not have to define us. By choosing to face and learn from the pain, we can heal, grow, and live more fully, honouring the pain and the lessons it brings. Emotional breakdowns are natural, not signs of weakness, and offering ourselves grace can be a powerful tool for recovery. Trauma and unhappiness can lead to profound personal development, but it requires time, reflection, support, and self-compassion.

CHAPTER 12

# LIVE LIKE A STOIC

*"No one can live happily who has regard for himself alone and transforms everything into a question of his own utility; you must live for your neighbour if you would live for yourself."*
*– Seneca*

Anxiety. The word alone can feel heavy, like a weight pressing down your chest. It creeps in when you least expect it—during a conversation, before a big event, or in the quiet moments when your mind should be at ease. It whispers doubts, magnifies fears, and sometimes makes the world feel just a little too overwhelming. But what if anxiety isn't just an obstacle? What if there are strengths worth embracing hidden within its restless energy?

Do you ever get anxiety? My sister was the first person to read this book when it was simply a guide. She is at the extreme end of the anxiety paradigm. The message I passed on to her is to begin with the silver lining of anxiety and not beat yourself up about it.

Think about it: Your mind is constantly analysing, preparing and anticipating. While others go through life unaware of what could go wrong, you've already mapped out every possibility, ensuring you're ready for whatever comes your way. You spot details that others miss. Whether it's an inconsistency in a story, a slight shift in someone's mood, or an opportunity disguised as a challenge, your heightened awareness helps you navigate life with a unique depth of understanding.

Your empathy runs deep. Anxiety makes you hyper-aware, of both your own emotions and of the feelings of those around you. You notice when a friend struggles, even when they insist they're fine. You listen intently, offering comfort and reassurance because you know what it's like to battle inner turmoil. That sensitivity is a gift—it makes you a loyal friend, a compassionate listener, someone people trust with their hearts.

And let's talk about your resilience. Every time you face your fears, push through the overthinking, or make it through a tough day, you prove your strength. Anxiety doesn't mean weakness; it means you've been carrying a heavier mental load and you're still standing. That's powerful.

Then there's creativity. Ever wonder why so many artists, writers and musicians struggle with anxiety? It's because their minds, like yours, constantly search, feel and question. Anxiety forces you to dig deep and explore emotions in a way that others might never experience. Your thoughts may race, but within them lies creativity, insight and originality that can lead to something truly remarkable.

Yes, anxiety is tough. It's frustrating, exhausting, and sometimes relentless. But it's also part of what makes you you—thoughtful, prepared, empathetic, resilient and creative. So next time anxiety tries to tell you that you're not enough, remind yourself of this: You are not just someone who struggles with anxiety. You are someone who thrives despite it. That's something to be proud of.

With all of this in mind, it's in your best interests to overcome debilitating episodes of anxiety and work towards cultivating positivity and overcoming negative thinking. Many people who have anxiety rely on cognitive behavioural therapy (CBT) as a form of treatment. Stoic philosophy profoundly influences CBT because it helps people reframe their thoughts and reactions to challenges.

To recap, Stoicism, an ancient Greek and Roman school of thought, emphasises that we do not suffer from events themselves, but from our interpretation of them—a core principle that aligns closely with CBT. The Stoic philosopher Epictetus famously said, "It's not what happens to you, but how you react to it that matters." Similarly, CBT teaches that negative emotions often stem from distorted thinking rather than external events. By identifying and challenging irrational thoughts, we can cultivate healthier perspectives.

Another key Stoic principle is the Dichotomy of Control, which we focused on in Chapter 2. It highlights the distinction between what is within your control (your thoughts, actions) and what is not (external events, other people's actions). CBT echoes this by encouraging people to focus on changing their thought patterns and behaviours instead of trying to control external circumstances. Additionally, Stoicism promotes cognitive reframing through *premeditatio malorum* (visualising worst-case scenarios), which helps us develop resilience by mentally preparing for adversity. CBT applies a similar approach to cognitive restructuring, where we learn to reframe negative or catastrophic thoughts into a more balanced, rational approach.

Mindfulness and emotional regulation are also central to both Stoicism and CBT. Marcus Aurelius advised, "You have power over your mind—not outside events. Realise this, and you will find strength." CBT incorporates mindfulness-based strategies to help people become aware of their automatic thoughts, allowing them to pause and respond thoughtfully rather than impulsively. Furthermore, Stoicism emphasises self-discipline and resilience, encouraging us to endure hardships with reason and maintain equanimity. CBT aligns with this by helping us develop coping strategies and practice gradual exposure to feared situations.

By drawing on Stoic principles, CBT equips us with practical tools to manage anxiety, depression and stress. Both the philosophy and the psychological treatment emphasise that while we cannot always control what happens to us, we can control how we interpret and respond to it, leading to greater mental wellbeing and emotional strength.

I am not promoting CBT as I have never engaged in the treatment, though I have been interested in its roots in Stoicism. I support the idea that your thoughts, feelings, physical sensations and actions are interconnected and that negative thoughts and feelings can trap you in a negative cycle. I have been there, and I know people in this trap. Cognitive behavioural therapy, or CBT, a psychological treatment that helps people identify and change these negative thought patterns and behaviours to improve their mental wellbeing, was born from Stoicism. This is validating for me. Stoicism has become such a strong scaffolding in my life, forming part of the structure for self-improvement and successfully elevating my baseline of happiness.

*****

I have kicked off this chapter with a focus on anxiety because it is something we all experience to some extent, as it is a feeling of worry, fear or unease. In many situations, it is a normal reaction to uncertain situations, such as taking a test, starting a new job, or facing a big decision. However, when anxiety becomes excessive and persistent and interferes with daily life, it may be classified as an anxiety disorder. My sister's level of anxiety dwarfs mine; I've had some full-blown panic attacks in my life, which were debilitating, but my anxiety has always been relatively manageable. I am well aware of and have experienced many of its symptoms, though, including excessive worry, restlessness, increased heart rate, rapid breathing, sweating, trouble concentrating, difficulty sleeping and stomach discomfort (which is where it always resides for me—right in the gut).

If anxiety becomes overwhelming or interferes with daily life, seeking support from a mental health professional can be helpful. I have done this, and it has helped. Even though my anxiety is rarely acute, I have also tried various ways to manage it, including therapy, lifestyle changes and mindfulness techniques. I have also tried medication.

In recent years, practising Stoicism has been a powerful tool for managing any form of anxiety I experience because it helps me shift my perspective, focusing on what I can control and letting go of what I cannot. I've learnt that external events are outside my control, but my reactions, thoughts, and judgements are within my power. By focusing only on what I can influence, I've been able to reduce unnecessary worry about things beyond my reach. I mentioned *premeditatio malorum* when discussing CBT. This practice seems to help where I imagine worst-case scenarios to lessen their emotional impact. Instead of fearing uncertainty, I mentally prepare for it, making real challenges feel more manageable when they arise.

I also live in the present moment rather than dwelling on past regrets or future anxieties. Marcus Aurelius often wrote about focusing on the "task at hand." I remind myself to do the same rather than get consumed by worry. I'm learning to live more in the present moment, resisting the pull of past regrets and future anxieties. Stoicism has also taught me to question my automatic negative thoughts. When anxiety creeps in, I ask myself, "Is this thought rational?" or "What's the worst that could happen?" This simple practice helps me break the cycle of anxious thinking. Another key lesson I've embraced is viewing adversity as an opportunity for growth. Instead of fearing difficulties, I see them as challenges that build resilience. Seneca said, "Difficulties strengthen the mind, as labour does the body."

Practising voluntary discomfort with simple things like taking cold plunges, swimming in the middle of winter, high-intensity interval training and going after challenging feats has also made a difference. By deliberately stepping outside my comfort zone, I've become less afraid of discomfort, which has made my anxiety feel less overwhelming. Lastly, journalling has been a valuable tool in my Stoic practice. As Marcus Aurelius wrote in his *Meditations*, to process thoughts, I use writing to reflect on my emotions and gain perspective. I've developed a more resilient mindset and calm by incorporating these Stoic principles into my life. I am better equipped to handle anxiety and the challenges of everyday living.

Whether you have never experienced any form of anxiety or whether it is mild, moderate or severe, I believe you can improve your position on the spectrum. The big-ticket items covered in individual chapters of this book will reduce anxiety while increasing your happiness. Nutrition, abandoning alcohol, moving and exercising, changing habits, and applying discipline to your life all help. Throw in living like a Stoic with the Dichotomy of Control, mindfulness and emotional regulation, *premeditatio malorum* and practising voluntary discomfort, and your emotional fitness will constantly improve.

Living like a Stoic is like stepping into the eye of a storm—while chaos swirls around you, you remain calm, anchored in reason and perspective. Anxiety thrives on uncertainty and the illusion of control, but Stoicism teaches you to release your grip on what you cannot change. Focusing only on your thoughts, actions and responses frees you from the exhausting need to micromanage the world. Instead of fearing the future, you embrace the present moment with resilience, seeing obstacles as opportunities for growth rather than threats. When you accept that setbacks, criticism, and even loss are inevitable parts of life, they lose their power to unnerve you. Like a sailor who trusts the strength of their vessel rather than fearing the waves, the Stoic mind finds peace—not in avoiding hardship, but in mastering the art of navigating it.

Although I can't find a direct reference, I once heard in a podcast that Viktor Frankl was a great admirer of Epictetus. Interestingly, we have more documentation from Epictetus than any other Stoic, thanks largely to the efforts of his student who preserved his teachings. I referenced Frankl's view on happiness in Chapter 2: "Happiness cannot be pursued; it must ensue, and it only does so as the unintended side-effect of one's dedication to a cause greater than oneself or as the by-product of one's surrender to a person other than oneself." This idea has deeply influenced my own desire to live in service of something greater than myself.

One of the most powerful aspects of Stoicism—though it took me years to truly engage with and put into practice—is its emphasis on our social responsibilities. The philosophy teaches that living a meaningful and fulfilling life isn't just about personal resilience or self-mastery, but also about contributing to the common good, serving others, and helping make the world a better place.

In Chapter 2, I discussed that Rome's most influential philosophical schools of thought are often associated with personal resilience, emotional control and rationality, to live like a Stoic. All of this is in the first half of this chapter. However, its social dimensions are equally significant. Far from being an isolated or self-centred philosophy, Stoicism emphasises our responsibility to others, the necessity of working for the common good, and the moral imperative to improve the world. By understanding and embracing this aspect of Stoic thought, you can find greater meaning and fulfilment in life, for yourself and society at large.

Stoicism teaches that human beings are naturally social creatures, interconnected with one another and bound by a shared rationality. The Stoics believed in oikeiosis, the natural inclination to care for others, starting with one's family and expanding outward to include all of humanity. This idea, championed by thinkers such as

Epictetus, Seneca and Marcus Aurelius, implies that personal virtue is incomplete without social responsibility.

Marcus Aurelius, in his *Meditations*, consistently reminds himself that he exists for the benefit of others. He writes, "That which is not good for the swarm, neither is it good for the bee." This metaphor illustrates that the individual's wellbeing is intrinsically linked to the community's wellbeing. True Stoic practice, therefore, demands that we recognise our duty to contribute positively to society through acts of kindness, service or justice.

A central tenet of Stoicism is that virtue is the highest good. In the Stoic sense, virtue is about personal integrity and fulfilling our societal roles with wisdom, courage, justice and temperance. Justice in particular refers to our relationships with others and calls us to act fairly, uphold truth and work for the common good.

Stoic philosophers argue that we must view ourselves as citizens of the world rather than just members of a specific nation, class or group. This cosmopolitan view, articulated by the Stoic thinker Hierocles, suggests that our moral duty extends beyond our immediate circles to encompass all of humanity. By actively participating in and improving our communities, we fulfil a greater purpose, aligning ourselves with nature's rational order.

Stoicism teaches that we are responsible for our moral progress and improving society. Seneca, for instance, advised that wisdom and knowledge are meaningless unless they are used to help others. A Stoic does not merely retreat into contemplation, but actively engages with the world, striving to correct injustices and alleviate suffering where possible.

Stoicism encourages working for the common welfare through leadership and public service. Despite his power as a Roman emperor, Marcus Aurelius viewed his role as a duty rather than a privilege. He constantly sought to govern with fairness, humility and a sense of responsibility to his people. This translates to ethical leadership, civic engagement and the pursuit of justice in various spheres of life, whether in politics, business or personal relationships.

The Stoics remind us that the world is neither inherently good nor bad; rather, it is shaped by individuals' actions. To live a meaningful life, we must contribute to improving the world. This does not necessarily mean grand gestures or dramatic acts of heroism—simple daily choices to act with kindness, integrity and generosity can have a profound impact. The Stoic philosopher Epictetus encouraged people to focus on what is within their control. While we may not be able to eradicate all suffering or injustice, we can take meaningful steps towards improving our immediate surroundings. This can include mentoring others, engaging in charitable work, advocating for truth and fairness, or simply treating others with respect and empathy.

Pursuing personal fulfilment is often misguided when seeking material wealth, power or transient pleasures. Stoicism offers a different perspective: true fulfilment arises from a life of virtue, service and contribution to the common good. By aligning our personal goals with the wellbeing of others, we cultivate more profound contentment and a sense of purpose. A significant life is not measured by status or external achievements, but by the positive impact one has on others. Whether through small acts of kindness or large-scale societal change, living according to Stoic principles ensures that our existence is meaningful and aligned with the greater good.

\*\*\*\*

I've always volunteered at events within the kids' schools, donated money to charity, been a regular blood donor and enjoyed cleaning up a little harbour beach near home. I have done some gratifying volunteer work by enriching the lives of people with disabilities by teaching them how to ski through a professional adaptive organisation. Still, I've wanted to do something substantial for my community for years. Timing for these commitments does play a role, as taking care of yourself is essential before you can effectively care for others. Just like a car needs fuel to run, you need to nourish your body, mind and emotions to be fully present for those who rely on you. If you neglect your wellbeing, stress and exhaustion can build up, making it harder to offer others support, patience and love. Prioritising self-care—whether through rest, healthy habits, or setting boundaries—ensures you have the energy and emotional balance to give your best to those around you. Remember, you can't pour from an empty cup. By looking after yourself first, you become stronger, more compassionate and better equipped to care for others. I learnt this the hard way.

With the kids taking more and more agency over their own lives, even though they are only 10 and 12, I recently reached a point where I finally had some capacity to apply time to something else. My bank balance told me to scale up my business to meet rising living costs and school fees. My brain told me to do some further tertiary education. My heart told me to spend time with family and friends, but my gut guided me to do something for others, my community, and my fellow man. Right about when my bank balance, brain, heart and gut were duking it out, an online philosophy group I am a part of was discussing Stoicism and the importance of contributing to society. For several years, I had been toying with ideas on what I could do for others. Something for the homeless, perhaps some skills-based support or mentoring, or a local charity or food bank, underprivileged kids or those with disabilities were my interests. One of the guys in my philosophy group was a volunteer for a crisis helpline. I got a sense of how integral such a service was to the community, directly impacting people in their most vulnerable moments. How a simple compassionate conversation can help someone feel heard, understood and less alone. By playing a role in preventing self-harm or suicide, or simply by offering emotional support, volunteers build a more resilient and connected community where people know they can reach out for help.

I started looking into Lifeline and was drawn to some key aspects of the service. Supporting help-seekers requires patience, understanding and non-judgement, things I know I could improve. Crisis support isn't about giving advice; it's about helping people find their own solutions and inner resilience, which can have a lasting impact on their wellbeing.

*"Waste no more time arguing what a good man should be. Be one."* – Marcus Aurelius

Deciding to work for Lifeline was not a decision I made lightly. I had always felt a deep sense of empathy for those struggling with mental health challenges, and I wanted to contribute to a cause that truly made a difference. I had often found myself as the person friends and family would turn to in times of need, and I realised that my ability to listen and provide comfort was something I could use to help on a broader scale. After much reflection, I realised that becoming a crisis supporter was the path that aligned with my values and desire to help others in their most vulnerable moments.

The training process was both rigorous and enlightening. The theory component introduced me to the fundamentals of crisis support, active listening, and the complexities of mental health crises. I learnt the importance of being non-judgemental, offering support without direct advice, and how to de-escalate situations. The practical training sessions were invaluable, allowing me to put my learning into practice through role-playing exercises and real-time feedback from experienced mentors. I was super nervous during the first role-playing sessions, fearing I wouldn't say the right thing or would fail to provide comfort. But with each session, my confidence grew, and I began to trust in the process.

Through this journey, I gained technical skills and grew personally. I developed a deeper understanding of human resilience and the power of genuine connection. The training reinforced the importance of self-care and boundaries, ensuring I could be present for help-seekers without becoming overwhelmed. I learnt to recognise my emotional limits and the importance of seeking support when needed. This experience has changed how I approach my relationships, making me a more patient and understanding friend and family member.

> "What is the first business of one who practices philosophy? To rid himself of self-conceit. For it is impossible for a man to begin to learn what he thinks he already knows." – Epictetus

The more I learnt, the less I felt I knew. Still, when the two-hour practical assessment arrived, all the hard work intersected to give me the skillset to handle several challenging role-play scenarios, graduate, and receive the accreditation needed to take help-seeker calls from people in a real crisis.

Then came the moment I had been preparing for—taking my first call as a crisis supporter. My heart raced as I logged in, unsure of what to expect. The call came through, and I took a deep breath before answering. The help-seeker on the other end was experiencing intense distress, and I leaned into my training, offering them a compassionate and safe space to express their emotions. As the conversation unfolded, I witnessed the profound impact of simply listening. It was an incredibly humbling experience to hear someone slowly shift from hopelessness to a place where they felt heard and understood. By the end of the call, they expressed gratitude for being listened to and supported. That moment solidified my belief in the work we do.

Some parts of the Lifeline support system feel unnatural, but the process works, and I trust it. As it becomes more natural for me, I will improve in the role.

Contributing to society in this way has given me a sense of purpose unlike anything else. Each call reminds me of the strength and vulnerability within us all. Being a crisis supporter for Lifeline is more than just volunteering; it is a commitment to being there for others in their darkest times, providing hope when they feel lost, and ensuring that no one has to face their struggles alone.

I am proud to be part of this vital service, knowing that every conversation has the potential to make a real difference in someone's life. It is compelling to be a steady presence for someone feeling lost or overwhelmed. Every call reminds me of the importance of human connection, and I carry that lesson with me in all aspects of my life. My journey with Lifeline has allowed me to help others and helped me grow into a more compassionate and self-aware person. This role has changed me in ways I never expected, and I am deeply grateful.

When I first signed up for Lifeline training, I expected to learn how to help others. What I didn't realise was how much the journey would help me. The 170 hours of training—an intricate blend of self-paced learning, role-plays, face-to-face sessions and call observations—sometimes felt like a juggling act. Between kids, work, life and the emotional weight of preparing to support people in crisis, I often wondered if I was absorbing enough and if I would be ready when the time came to take my first real call. And then, suddenly, training was over. The hours spent navigating challenging conversations with trainers and fellow trainees, the moments of doubt and growth, and the deepening of empathy and active listening skills became part of me. The memory of the effort faded, but the impact remained. Long before I sat at the phone console for the first time, I realised I had already received far more than I had given. I had gained a new way of listening—not just hearing words but genuinely understanding what lay beneath them. I had learnt to sit with discomfort, to hold space for another person's pain without rushing to fix it. I had been given the privilege of connection, and the realisation that simply being present can be the greatest gift of all.

And perhaps most unexpectedly, I had become more aware of my own emotions, my own needs, and my resilience. When my first shift finally arrived, I wasn't the same person who had nervously clicked "enrol" all those months ago. Of course, I still felt the butterflies of uncertainty, but I also felt something else—trust. Trust in the training that had shaped me. Trust in the support of my mentors and fellow crisis supporters. Trust in the power of simply being there for another human being. The caller didn't know it was my first shift. They didn't realise the countless hours of preparation, the personal growth, and the late nights spent practising de-escalation techniques in my head. All they knew was that someone was there, willing to listen. And in that moment, nothing else mattered.

Becoming a crisis supporter isn't just about giving—it's about growing. It's about becoming more present, open and connected to the world. I set out to support others, but in doing so, I found that I was supported too. That is the true gift of this journey.

My Stoic journey took on a different path as soon as I stepped into Lifeline's Northern Beaches Call Centre. I had moved past what initially drew me to Stoicism, the attraction to managing my emotions, being disciplined, more balanced and courageous. This self-centred version of Stoicism was a game changer, but giving was much more profound. Trophies, championships, degrees and job success don't even get a look-in. Knowing that I've been there for someone during their darkest hour is deeply meaningful—perhaps one of the most rewarding experiences of my life.

There are small and large experiences like this out there for everyone. Experiences whereby in giving, you get more back.

## REMEMBER THIS

Stoicism is more than a philosophy of personal endurance; it guides ethical living and social responsibility. By recognising our duty to others, working for the common welfare and striving to improve the world, we contribute to society's wellbeing and achieve personal fulfilment. In a world that often encourages self-interest, Stoicism reminds us that true significance comes from service, justice and the relentless pursuit of virtue. In embracing these ideals, we live better lives and leave a lasting, positive legacy for those who come after us.

Imagine a world where we lived for each other and not ourselves. It doesn't have to be a big commitment; it doesn't have to be right now, but include others in your plans. As Seneca said, "Wherever there is a human being, there is an opportunity for kindness."

CHAPTER 13

# LET GO OF EVERYTHING THAT IS BLOCKING YOUR HAPPINESS

*"Letting go involves being aware of a feeling, letting it come up, staying with it, and letting it run its course without wanting to make it different or do anything about it."*
— Dr Hawkins

There wasn't one, single, precise reason for bottoming right out and hitting a level of deep depression. I felt I had been dealing with the trauma of losing Lou very well, but in hindsight, I think I was helping the kids deal with the trauma and neglecting myself. They had their scheduled grief counselling, I was always asking them about their feelings, and I was always finding relevant ways for them to process losing their mum. I didn't do much of this for myself. Perhaps when I decided to commit to another relationship three years after losing Lou, and it didn't work out, I struggled with the rejection and the feeling of abandonment.

Losing a spouse is a harrowing experience, and even though they didn't choose to leave, it can still feel like abandonment. This feeling arises because, in many ways, your partner was an anchor in your life—someone who provided love, support and companionship.

When they pass away, especially if it happens suddenly, it can feel like they've left you behind to face life alone.

Grief is not always rational, and emotions don't always align with logic. Your mind may know they didn't want to go, but your heart still feels the emptiness and loneliness of their absence. The routines you shared, the unspoken understanding between you, and the simple presence of someone who truly knew you—losing all of that at once can make it feel like they disappeared, leaving you to navigate life without them.

On a deeper level, abandonment isn't just about someone choosing to leave—it's about the impact of their absence. When a loved one dies, the security and stability they provide are suddenly gone. You may feel lost, unprotected and unsure of how to move forward, much like someone abandoned. The pain of grief can also bring up unresolved emotions, fears or past wounds, intensifying the feeling that you've been left behind.

Recognising that this feeling is a natural part of grief is essential. It doesn't mean you're ungrateful for the love you shared or that you don't understand the circumstances. It simply means that loss is profound, and when someone so central to your life is gone, their absence can feel like an unbearable void—one that, at times, resembles abandonment.

****

I appeared to manage very well for several years after Lou's death, but then I spiralled fast, and I felt horrible very quickly. It was a feeling of being trapped in a fog that wouldn't lift, a heavy weight pressing down on my chest, making even the simplest tasks feel impossible. No matter how much I slept, I woke up exhausted, and every day felt like I was dragging myself through quicksand. I felt hollow, even when I was surrounded by people who cared.

My mind whispered cruel lies—telling me I wasn't enough, that I didn't matter, that things would never get better. The world had lost colour, and joy felt like a distant memory, something meant for others but never for me. I wanted to reach out and tell someone, but the words stuck in my throat. I didn't want to bother anyone with my problems. Even when someone asked if I was okay, I forced a smile because explaining felt harder than suffering in silence. It was a battle between wanting to be seen and fearing I was invisible, between hoping for relief and doubting it would ever come. But deep inside, there was a tiny ember—a part of me that still longed for light, hoped and fought, even when it felt like there was nothing besides the kids left to fight for.

I grabbed onto that ember so it didn't get snuffed out. A single book was a massive help in that time of despair. In the introduction, I mentioned that my sister handed me a transformative guide that explores the power of releasing attachments and surrendering to the flow of life for greater emotional freedom. This book was the first influence to magnetise my inner compass needle in the right direction and help move me out of the hole I resided in.

****

*Letting Go: The Pathway of Surrender* is authored by Dr David R. Hawkins. As a renowned psychiatrist, spiritual teacher, and author, Dr Hawkins brings a wealth of knowledge and experience to his exploration of letting go as a powerful pathway to personal and spiritual growth. His suggestions positively affected me and involved surrendering my ego's attachments, desires and negative emotions, leading to greater inner peace and spiritual realisation. The book delves into the theory and provides practical insights and techniques for letting go. It guides readers on embracing acceptance, forgiveness and mindfulness, empowering them to take control of their emotional wellbeing. Dr Hawkins's application emphasises that surrendering to the present moment and releasing resistance can lead to profound spiritual and personal transformation.

After reading the book, I practised his teaching daily. I have summarised his guide for you; it's as simple as it reads and easy to do. It will help you break free from the limitations of your ego, overcome emotional suffering, and experience a deeper connection with your true self and the world around you. Practice this with your very next negative emotion

**Awareness and acceptance:** Begin by becoming aware of your emotions, thoughts and feelings. This is often instantaneous, as certain negative feelings can rage. However, I also have anxious feelings that arise and catch me off guard, for no perceived reason. Acknowledge and accept these feelings without judgement. This involves being honest with yourself about what you are experiencing.

**Feel the emotion:** Allow yourself to feel the emotion without resistance. Experience it without trying to suppress, deny or amplify it. Let the emotion flow through you without attachment.

**Identify the sensations:** Pay attention to any physical sensations associated with the emotion. These could include tension in the body, a knot in the stomach, a chaotic brain or other bodily reactions. Occasionally, this acknowledgement makes me feel physically sick, as the feeling rises from the pit of my stomach, through my oesophagus, and wants to exit my mouth physically. Identify and observe these sensations without judgement.

**Resist the urge to label:** Refrain from labelling the emotion as good, bad or ugly. Instead, view it as a passing experience. Recognise that emotions are temporary and do not define who you are.

**Ask yourself, "Could I let this go?":** Ask yourself if you are willing to let go of the emotion. This is not about *forcing* yourself to let go, but being open to the possibility. The question is an invitation to release the attachment to the emotion.

**Choose to let go:** Make a conscious decision to let go of the emotion. This involves a willingness to surrender and release the grip that the emotion has on you. It's not about suppressing or denying the emotion, but about dissipating it. I understand that sometimes a feeling is so acute because negative emotions are so powerful and painful that they may not go away. In these situations, it may be necessary to make additional attempts, without ever forcing the issue.

**Feel the release:** As you choose to let go, observe any shifts in your emotional state. You may feel a sense of relief, lightness or clarity. Allow yourself to experience the release without expectation. Hopefully, you get a depressurising feeling of some type.

**Repeat as necessary:** The letting go process can be repeated as needed. It's a tool that can be applied to various emotions and situations. Over time and with practice, releasing emotions as they arise may become more natural. This has been the case for me, especially for day-to-day negative feelings. I use it for minor things, like when someone cuts me off or fails to acknowledge that I've created a space for them in bumper-to-bumper traffic. I have used the technique for many big feelings: accidents, loss, failure, embarrassment, disappointment, fears, work deadlines, public speaking, sadness, anger and frustration. It does work.

That is it. The process is easy; the outcomes may take time, but make it a habit. Consciously do it daily for the next 90 days, and it will become routine.

Dr Hawkins emphasises that the letting go technique is not a form of repression or suppression, but rather a way to allow emotions to pass through without creating unnecessary suffering. The goal is to move towards inner peace and higher consciousness. Who doesn't want that, right? The process was pivotal in helping me work through my emotional trauma and then slowly enhancing my happiness.

The core of Hawkins's method involves acknowledging and experiencing emotions fully without suppression or avoidance. Doing so can release pent-up emotions, leading to emotional freedom. This liberation from emotional baggage allows for a more balanced and joyful mind. Holding onto negative emotions such as anger, fear and resentment contributes significantly to stress and anxiety. Letting go helps dissolve these negative emotional states, reducing overall stress and creating a more peaceful and relaxed mental state. When negative emotions are released, mental clutter diminishes. This will result in you having greater mental clarity, improved focus, and enhanced decision-making abilities.

Letting go of grievances and judgements improves interpersonal relationships. By releasing adverse emotional reactions, you can interact more harmoniously with others, fostering deeper connections and mutual respect, which are vital components of happiness. Hawkins's process encourages alignment with higher levels of consciousness, characterised by peace, love and joy. Letting go of lower vibrational emotions naturally elevates an individual's emotional state, making you more receptive to positive experiences and inner joy. Letting go is empowering because it puts you in control of your emotional wellbeing. This self-empowerment encourages continuous personal growth and the pursuit of meaningful goals, contributing to a sustained sense of happiness.

Letting go has become part of my spiritual journey. It involves surrendering to the inconsistent flow of life. If you mentioned my name and "spiritual journey" in the same sentence a couple of years ago, I would have fallen off my chair. This technique, combined with the other recommendations in this book, is leading me to more profound spiritual insights and a deeper sense of purpose and connection, enhancing my overall happiness. Letting go equips us with the resilience to handle life's inevitable challenges more easily. By not clinging to negative emotions, we can navigate complex situations more positively and proactively, maintaining happiness even in adversity.

Here are some practical examples of emotions you might consider letting go of according to his process.

**Anger:** This is one emotion for which I have never seen a positive outcome. This emotion can be destructive to oneself and relationships with others. Letting go of anger involves recognising it, understanding its roots, and then releasing the need to hold onto it

**Fear:** Fear often prevents people from pursuing their true potential and enjoying life. Releasing fear can lead to greater freedom and a more fulfilling life.

**Guilt:** Carrying guilt can weigh heavily on the mind and spirit. Letting go of guilt involves forgiving oneself and others and understanding that everyone makes mistakes.

**Shame:** This is a deep-seated emotion that can undermine self-worth and confidence. Releasing shame requires self-acceptance and self-compassion.

**Pride:** While some pride can be healthy, excessive pride can prevent personal growth and strain relationships. Letting go of pride involves humility and openness to learning from others.

**Resentment:** Holding onto resentment keeps wounds open and prevents healing. Letting go of resentment means forgiving those who have wronged us, not for their sake, but for our peace.

**Jealousy:** This emotion can corrode relationships and personal happiness. Letting go of jealousy involves developing a sense of gratitude for what one has and recognising the uniqueness of one's journey.

**Grief:** While natural, prolonged grief can hinder moving forward. Letting go of grief involves honouring the loss and then gradually finding ways to embrace life again. For the most part, it took me almost five years to let go of this emotion; however, some days I am still letting go.

**Hopelessness:** This emotion can lead to stagnation and a lack of motivation. Releasing hopelessness involves finding faith in oneself and the future, even in small, incremental ways.

**Desire:** Unfulfilled desires can lead to a constant state of dissatisfaction. Letting go of obsessive desires involves cultivating contentment with the present moment and with what one already has.

At the time of writing this book, I often find myself letting go of my lifelong feelings of impostor syndrome, where I feel doubt about my intellect, skills or accomplishments among the high-achieving individuals in my circle, sporting interests, or business ventures.

I initially used this technique to manage intense emotions, including rejection, resentment, grief and anger, but I eventually turned it into a habit through daily, small interactions.

At first glance, the letting go technique might appear to conflict with the principles of Stoicism. Both aim to cultivate inner peace and emotional balance, but they arise from different philosophical foundations and offer distinct methods for navigating life's challenges.

Stoicism, rooted in ancient Greek philosophy and founded by Zeno of Citium in the 3rd century BCE, teaches that the path to a good life lies in living virtuously and rationally. It emphasises aligning with nature (reason), accepting what we cannot control, and managing our responses to external events. Through practice and perspective, Stoicism helps build a resilient mind that can remain steady in the face of adversity.

In contrast, the letting go technique draws from modern psychology and spiritual insight. It centres on the idea that emotions are energies that can be fully felt and surrendered, rather than analysed or resisted. Through this surrender, we move towards greater emotional freedom and higher states of consciousness. While Stoicism seeks mastery over one's thoughts and reactions through reason, the letting go method bypasses the intellect and works directly with the emotional experience itself.

When it comes to acceptance, the differences are even more apparent. Stoicism teaches rational detachment. It's famous Dichotomy of Control reminds us to focus only on what we can influence—our thoughts, actions and choices—and to let go of everything else. Acceptance, in the Stoic view, is grounded in perspective and mental discipline. The letting go approach, by contrast, encourages full emotional presence. Acceptance here means surrendering to the feeling in the moment without resistance, suppression or judgement. Rather than detaching from emotion, it invites us to feel it entirely until it dissolves on its own.

The two practices also differ in their tools and techniques. Stoicism offers structured mental practices such as daily reflection, *premeditatio malorum* (visualising potential hardships), and *amor fati*—a wholehearted embrace of whatever life brings. These help cultivate resilience, humility and strength of character. The letting go technique is more fluid and experiential. Rather than thinking through challenges, it involves observing emotional sensations as they arise, staying with them without clinging or pushing them away. As Hawkins suggests, the emotion will naturally dissolve when fully felt, revealing a deeper state of calm.

Ultimately, Stoicism aims to live a virtuous life aligned with reason and integrity, finding tranquillity through wisdom and self-control. Letting go, on the other hand, is a pathway towards emotional liberation, higher consciousness, and even spiritual awakening. For me, these approaches don't contradict each other—they complement one another beautifully. Stoicism gives me clarity, structure, and strength. The letting go technique allows me to process emotions that reason alone can't always reach. Depending on the situation, the feelings involved and the time I have, I'll choose one approach or combine both.

There are many situations where this balance is especially powerful. When dealing with criticism or rejection, for example, Stoicism offers a calm, rational stance. It reminds me that I can control my response but not others' opinions. From a Stoic viewpoint, I might reflect on whether the criticism is useful, let go of the rest, and move forward with dignity. But if the criticism triggers strong emotions like shame or anger, the letting go technique becomes valuable. Instead of repressing or justifying those feelings, I allow myself to feel them fully, without judgement. In doing so, I release emotional tension and return to a clearer, more grounded state.

Grief and loss is another area where both approaches shine. Stoicism teaches me to honour impermanence, to be grateful for what was, and to accept that all things pass. It helps me keep perspective and find peace in life's natural cycles. Yet grief is rarely just an intellectual experience—it comes in waves of sadness, longing and pain. The letting go technique helps me meet those waves without fear. By allowing myself to feel deeply, I give space for the emotions to move through me, preventing suppression or stagnation. This creates a pathway for authentic healing.

When facing anxiety or fear about the future, Stoicism helps ground me. I ask: "Is this within my control?" If not, I redirect my focus to present actions. Negative visualisation—imagining the worst-case scenario—helps reduce my fear of the unknown by preparing me mentally. But sometimes, anxiety isn't rational. It shows up in the body: tight chest, racing thoughts, unease. That's when letting go is more effective. I stop trying to think my way out of it and sit with the feeling instead. By doing nothing but allowing it to be felt, I let the fear release itself.

In moments of anger or resentment, Stoicism invites me to reframe the situation. Did I have unrealistic expectations? Was I demanding control over something I never owned? A Stoic would step back and see things from a broader, more detached perspective—what's called "viewing from above." But if anger is intense, rational thinking may not be enough. The letting go technique steps in here. Rather than arguing with the emotion, I feel it—fully and honestly—until it softens. Often, this reveals deeper wounds beneath the surface, allowing for more meaningful growth.

Even during major life changes—like job loss, relocation or relationship transitions—both methods offer support. Stoicism encourages me to accept change as part of life's rhythm and to focus on what's within my control, such as building new skills or reframing setbacks as opportunities. *Amor fati* helps me embrace the change itself. Yet big transitions often stir complex emotions: fear, sadness, frustration, even excitement. The letting go technique helps me process those layers, easing the internal turbulence and allowing me to adjust more peacefully.

Minor daily frustrations benefit from this dual approach. Stoicism reminds me that small annoyances are opportunities to practice patience and resilience. I can choose my response and not let trivial issues steal my peace. But if tension starts to accumulate—those little irritations that build up throughout the day—the letting go technique offers a quick reset. Instead of pushing them aside, I take a moment to release the emotional charge. This keeps my inner space clear and light.

Each method brings its wisdom. Stoicism equips me to reframe, reason and rise above. Letting go helps me release, feel, and return to presence. In my experience, both practices are indispensable. I don't see them as competing philosophies, but as two sides of the same coin—each offering a different way to return to stillness, clarity and peace.

## REMEMBER THIS

Let's round out this chapter by reiterating the process of letting go, as summarised from Dr Hawkins' book, *The Pathway to Surrender*.

It's about being aware of a feeling, letting it come up, staying with it and letting it run its course. Without wanting to make it different or do anything about it.

Let the feeling be there and focus on releasing the energy behind it.

Allow having the feeling without resisting it, venting it, fearing it.

It's just a feeling. Be with the feeling. Don't try to modify it.

Let go of wanting to resist the feeling. It may shift to another feeling, but the idea is that those feelings should become lighter.

The feeling will disappear, and the energy behind it dissipates.

When letting go, ignore all the thoughts and focus on the feeling itself.

The feeling could well return, and big, troubling feelings surely will, but if you continuously let them go the feeling will become lighter and the idea is eventually it will be gone.

A lot of this has to do with your own ego, so it can take time. You may even have to let go of the fear of attempting the process itself.

Let. Go.

CHAPTER 14

# WORK ON YOUR PURPOSE

There is some great literature on purpose, such as:
- *Man's Search for Meaning* by Viktor E. Frankl
- *The Purpose Driven Life* by Rick Warren
- *Start with Why* by Simon Sinek
- *The Seven Habits of Highly Effective People* by Stephen R. Covey

The most recent I've read after going down the blue zone rabbit hole is *Ikigai: The Japanese Secret to a Long and Happy Life* by Héctor García and Francesc Miralles.

Many of these books share a common theme that can help you on your path to discovering your purpose. One thing I have made significant progress in over the last few years is gaining deep self-awareness, motivated by a combination of literature and who I manifest to be. This means taking the time to honestly reflect on my core values—what principles matter most to me—as well as my passions and interests, the activities that bring me a sense of life, fulfilment or deep engagement; evaluating and deeply considering my strengths and talents, the things I'm naturally good at or have developed and truly enjoy using.

Most importantly, I'm paying attention to what gives my life meaning—those moments when I've felt most useful, proud or connected to something greater than myself. Without this inner clarity, my sense of purpose could be shaped by external expectations instead of what truly resonates with me. By understanding myself on this deeper level, I can begin to align my actions, goals and relationships with a purpose that feels authentic and energising.

I mentioned in Chapter 4 when discussing discipline that my purpose is centred around living a life of virtue through personal growth, loving parenthood and positive influence—nurturing my children with presence and care, inspiring others with compassion and authenticity, and creating a balanced, fulfilling life grounded in what is essential and enough.

I shared with you an evolving piece of content that I read most days:

My purpose is to be the best version of myself, nurture my children, set an example they not only respect but emulate, give them all the love and attention they need, radiate calmness and positive energy that's felt by those around me, and authentically influence others. Hence, they become better versions of themselves. I believe in the power of love, support, and understanding, and I aim to create a warm, caring environment where those around me can flourish—showing compassion, empathy, and generosity, spreading love and kindness in everything I do. To inspire and educate others, helping them discover their passions and achieve their full potential. I strive to be a positive influence and a source of knowledge, always encouraging growth and lifelong learning. I am committed to pursuing personal growth and happiness. To continually challenge myself, explore new interests, and cultivate a life filled with joy, fulfilment, and balance.

My priority is to have what is essential, and second, to have what is enough. Essentials include feeding my children healthy food, clothing them, providing them with warm, comfortable shelter, and every opportunity in education and co-curricular activities. It is affording the time to be present in their lives. Having enough is holidaying as a family once a year and continuing to live a balanced life where work and play are equal. If I live a life of virtue, my success and happiness will ensue.

To elaborate further on this, the biggest motivator for me in the decisions I make today and the intentions I set for myself is the grandfather I strive to be. My purpose is rooted in how I envision myself in my eighties. Apart from being incredibly active, I want my 80-year-old self to be marked by wisdom, warmth and humility. To carry the depth of a life well lived, offering insight not through preaching but through gentle storytelling and thoughtful example. Calm and grounded, I respond to life's challenges with composure and perspective, creating a peaceful presence that soothes and steadies those around me. I strive to be loving and present, giving my full attention to my family, especially my grandchildren, and offering them unconditional love and genuine interest in their lives. Empathetic and supportive, I listen with compassion, seek to understand without judgement, and uplift others simply by being a safe, affirming presence. My optimism and gratitude shine through in my appreciation of small moments and my ability to find joy in the present, helping others see the good in life. Even at 80, I remain curious and open-minded, committed to learning and growth, and I hope to model the value of lifelong curiosity. With a light-hearted sense of humour, I bring ease and connection to those around me without ever being dismissive. Most importantly, I aim to live with integrity, kindness, and humility—earning the respect and admiration of others and quietly inspiring them to become better versions of themselves.

Living with purpose often involves setting meaningful goals, aligning actions with values and striving towards a better version of oneself—both now and in the future. This forward-facing orientation keeps us motivated, hopeful and intentional in our choices. However, purpose isn't just about where you're going; it's also grounded in where you've come from.

Reflecting on your past—especially the challenges you've overcome, the habits you've broken, the growth you've experienced—provides context, humility and a sense of progress. It reminds you that you are not static, that change is possible, and that you are capable of transformation. Acknowledging your past gives depth to your present and fuels resilience for the future.

In this way, your purpose becomes more rooted, authentic and personal. It's not just a vision of who you want to be, it's also an affirmation of how far you've already come. The past becomes not a weight, but a foundation. Reflection fosters gratitude, reinforces your "why", and strengthens your commitment to continue moving forward.

When I look in the review mirror at the extended times I have resided below happy, I speculate the primary reasons are either a physiological reason, alcohol consumption or not having a purpose.

I will never definitively know the first potential reason: physiological. Concussions or even something as complex as my gut microbiome due to my diet may have played a role in my subpar mental health. I am very interested in the correlation between happiness and the branch of biology that deals with my normal functions as a living organism. While it is challenging to discern moods and emotions when examining the past, I continue to explore this topic with a more present-day focus.

You can set up your little control environments and test the effects of exercise, diet, mindfulness and sleep on your mood, concentration, energy and love. I do this today and enjoy the experimental process of making an observation, forming a hypothesis, changing behaviour and analysing my results. It's an effective here-and-now strategy for a better healthspan. You can gain knowledge and inspiration from all the research conducted in any area of interest, from epidemiological and observational studies to meta-analyses of randomised controlled trials. Then, do a personal case report on a change in an ingredient to see if you feel better.

If one of your intentions that makes up your purpose is to make a positive change to your mood, work through testing the removal of possible causes, one at a time, starting with the things you put in your mouth.

**Refined sugar:** Sources are soft drinks, lollies, baked goods
**Effect:** Causes blood sugar spikes and crashes, linked to mood swings and irritability.

**Highly processed foods:** Instant noodles, frozen dinners, chips
**Effect:** Often low in nutrients and high in additives that may negatively impact mood and brain health.

**Trans fats:** sources are packaged snacks, margarine, fried fast food
**Effect:** Increases inflammation and may negatively affect brain function.

**Excess caffeine:** sources are energy drinks, excessive coffee
**Effect:** Can increase anxiety, restlessness and sleep problems.

**Alcohol**
**Effect:** Depresses the central nervous system, potentially disrupting serotonin balance and sleep patterns.

This is simply a start. There is so much more to explore.

****

Writing this book has been a massive driver for me to look further within. When I began this journey in 2022, I had to look inside myself to make the necessary changes. But to write about it in a way that helps others, I went deeper. I engaged fully in introspection and self-reflection, examining my thoughts, emotions, motivations and behaviours. I explored my inner self to gain a deeper understanding of who I am, what drives me, and how I respond to various situations.

I needed to recognise variations in my mental and emotional state, my strengths and weaknesses, and my values and beliefs. Reflecting on my feelings and emotions helped me understand why I feel a certain way and how those feelings impact my behaviour and decisions. I need to be present, fully engage with my thoughts and emotions without judgement, and recognise recurring thoughts, behaviours and emotional responses to understand underlying patterns and triggers. Using insights from self-reflection to make positive changes, I can improve my relationships and develop a more fulfilling life. Addressing and resolving past traumas or negative experiences, accepting myself for who I am, including my flaws and imperfections, and striving to live in alignment with my true self, values and desires rather than conforming to external expectations. Looking within also involves exploring my spiritual beliefs and seeking a deeper connection with something greater than myself.

While looking within is a continuous and dynamic process that has led to greater self-understanding, emotional resilience and personal fulfilment, it has helped me understand why I may or may not have been functioning at my happiness potential during specific periods of my life. Alcohol is something that I turned off. The benefit was instant and continues to improve over time. Consistent alcohol abuse was undoubtedly a reason for not feeling good. It was one of three primary ingredients lowering my happiness level. I have proved that to myself.

Apart from possible physiological reasons and excessive alcohol consumption, the overarching conclusion I have reached for why I was merely existing through parts of my life and not living, is a lack of purpose. For 20 years of my life, I didn't have an inner radar. I was incredibly goal-driven in my early twenties. I also successfully achieved my goals, but I needed to learn the difference between having goals and having a purpose. Only through experience and self-reflection have I come to understand that the distinction between having goals and having a purpose lies in their scope, nature and impact on my life.

Goals are needed in life because they are specific. They are time-bound, with clear direction, action-oriented, and detailed in their planning and execution, with a focus on achievement. However, they are incredibly different from having a purpose. Purpose has a broader, overarching direction or meaning in life; it's more abstract and less quantifiable than goals. It's timeless— ongoing and enduring, potentially lasting a lifetime. It's inspiration-driven, providing a sense of meaning and motivation and serving as a guiding principle that influences decisions and actions. It's fulfilment-focused, a contribution to something larger than oneself.

Purpose reflects a person's core values and passions. While the difference between goals and purpose may be evident to you, it took me 45 years to work this out, ponder my purpose, and align myself with one.

Of course, there is a relationship between goals and purpose. Goals should ideally align with one's purpose. Purpose directs goal-setting, ensuring the goals are meaningful and contribute to the larger picture. For example, if your purpose is to promote education, your goals might include obtaining a degree in education, starting a teaching career, or creating educational content. A clear purpose can sustain motivation even when goals are challenging or setbacks occur. It provides a more profound reason to persevere.

While specific goals may change over time as circumstances and achievements evolve, purpose remains relatively constant, providing a stable foundation.

Goals are specific targets to achieve, while purpose is the broader reason for pursuing those targets. Goals provide milestones along the journey, whereas purpose offers the direction and meaning that make the trip worthwhile.

When it comes to goals, my exploration of literature has also helped me understand the difference between two distinct types of motivation that drive behaviour and actions: intrinsic and extrinsic motivation. Understanding the difference between them and recognising the importance of inherent goals is crucial for personal growth and sustained fulfilment.

Intrinsic motivation is engaging in activities for their own sake, out of genuine interest, enjoyment or satisfaction. This type of motivation is driven by internal rewards, such as personal growth, a sense of achievement, or the pleasure derived from the activity. This is a primary reason why I developed my 50by50 goals. Critical characteristics of intrinsic motivation include performing an activity voluntarily, without external pressure; a desire to improve skills and achieve competence in a particular area; and finding meaning and value in the activity itself. Examples of intrinsic motivation include reading a book because you love the story, playing a musical instrument for the joy it brings, or engaging in a hobby that you find deeply satisfying.

Extrinsic motivation, on the other hand, involves performing activities to obtain external rewards or avoid adverse outcomes. External factors, such as money, praise, grades or approval from others, drive this type of motivation. Key characteristics of extrinsic motivation include performing tasks for tangible rewards or incentives, engaging in activities to avoid punishment or negative consequences, and seeking approval, status or acknowledgment from others. Examples of extrinsic motivation include working primarily for the pay cheque, studying to get good grades, or participating in a competition to win prizes. While extrinsic motivation can achieve short-term goals, intrinsic motivation is generally more sustainable and fulfilling in the long run.

Having intrinsic goals is essential because activities driven by intrinsic motivation are more likely to keep you engaged and committed, as they align with your interests and values. Pursuing intrinsic goals leads to higher satisfaction and wellbeing, as the rewards are deeply personal and meaningful. Intrinsic motivation helps build resilience, as we are more likely to persist through challenges when we are personally invested in the activity. Focusing on inherent goals leads to personal growth and development, as the emphasis is on mastery and self-improvement rather than external validation. Intrinsically motivated individuals are often more creative and innovative, driven by curiosity and a genuine interest in exploring new ideas.

While intrinsic motivation is crucial for long-term fulfilment, extrinsic motivation can still play a role in achieving specific goals. The key is to find a balance between the two. For example, extrinsic rewards can initially motivate us to engage in an activity. Still, the ultimate goal should be to foster intrinsic motivation by making the activity enjoyable, meaningful and aligned with personal values. Intrinsic and extrinsic motivation serve different purposes, and recognising the importance of inherent goals can lead to a more fulfilling and engaged life. By focusing on activities that bring personal satisfaction and align with your values, you can achieve greater wellbeing and long-term success aligned with your purpose.

The Stoic philosophy has helped me with my intrinsic objectives and offers a profound approach to discovering and embracing one's purpose in life, intertwining reflection, gratitude and purposeful action. The timeless wisdom in the writings of Seneca and Marcus

Aurelius provides invaluable reminders that purpose is not merely a distant objective to be attained, but a daily practice of intentional living grounded in virtue and mindfulness. By absorbing and applying these Stoic teachings, we can navigate life's journey with greater clarity and direction, making decisions that align with our deepest values and contribute meaningfully to the greater good.

In a contemporary society often consumed by the pursuit of external validation and superficial success, the Stoic view on purpose is a vital counterbalance. It encourages us to return to our internal moral compass and commit to self-improvement and personal integrity. These insights challenge us to live with a purpose that transcends mere ambition, urging us towards a life imbued with wisdom and genuine understanding. Embracing the Stoic approach means cultivating a mindset that prioritises inner growth over outward achievements. Reflection allows us to assess and align our actions with our core principles. Gratitude keeps us grounded, reminding us to appreciate the present and recognise abundance in our lives. Action, informed by reflection and appreciation, propels us forward, enabling us to live each day with intention and make a meaningful impact.

As we navigate the complexities of life, let the wisdom of Epictetus, Seneca and Aurelius serve as a beacon, guiding us towards a purpose that is both deeply fulfilling and inherently meaningful. Their teachings remind us that true purpose is found not in fleeting success, but in the steadfast pursuit of a virtuous life lived with awareness and intentionality. By following this path, we can create a legacy of wisdom and virtue, contributing to the wellbeing of ourselves and the world around us.

- What are you most grateful for?
- What are you most proud of?
- What challenges you the most?

- What do you want more of?
- What do you want less of?
- What do you need to let go of?

Finding your purpose in life is not a straightforward path. It's not like assembling furniture or following a recipe—there's no clear set of instructions, no guaranteed steps that will lead you to an answer. It's messy, uncertain and deeply personal. And that's precisely what makes it so meaningful.

The truth is, your story is still unfolding. You are not a finished product, and that's a good thing. Every chapter, twist and turn adds depth to who you are. You may feel lost or unsure of where you're going right now. That doesn't mean you're failing; it simply means your story is still being written. There is wisdom in waiting, searching and not knowing. If you haven't yet found your purpose, don't panic. Start by finding something that inspires you. Inspiration is a spark—it might not light up your entire path, but it can guide your next step. Follow that curiosity. It could be a cause, a hobby, a feeling or even a person. Moving towards what lights you up is essential, even if it doesn't yet make perfect sense.

To do this, you'll need to step outside your comfort zone. That means saying yes to things that scare you a little. Growth lives in discomfort. But over time, discomfort becomes familiar. You realise that uncertainty isn't the enemy—it's a doorway. When you challenge yourself, you build confidence in your ability to navigate the unknown. Think about your future. Where do you want to be in five years? Who do you hope to become? And if that's hard to picture, try zooming out: who do you want to be when you're 80, 90 or even 100? What kind of stories do you want to tell? What kind of impact do you hope to have made? Vision gives your journey direction. It doesn't have to be crystal clear, but having a sense of who your best self is can help you take steps towards becoming them.

## **REMEMBER THIS**

You are unique. You have preferences, experiences, quirks and talents that nobody else does. Use them. Your purpose doesn't have to look like anyone else's, because your life doesn't. You already know what excites you and what drains you. Trust that knowledge. There's power in the things you love. They're clues to your calling. The more you connect with what energises you, the more naturally motivation and meaning will follow. You are not a passive observer in your life. You are deeply connected to the world and have the energy to give. The question is: where will you give it?

One of the most powerful ways to uncover your purpose is to care for your body and mind. When you're mentally clear and physically strong, it's easier to hear your voice. You'll have more resilience to handle setbacks and more capacity to explore new paths. Your purpose isn't out there waiting to be discovered. It's inside you, waiting for you to be ready to meet it. So, no—finding your purpose isn't easy. But it's not supposed to be. It's a lifelong process, one that evolves as you do. Start where you are. Stay curious. Get uncomfortable. Follow what inspires you. And trust that even when you feel lost, you are still moving forward.

CHAPTER 15

## STITCH IT ALL TOGETHER

*"Well-being is attained little by little,
and nevertheless is no little thing itself."*
— Zeno of Citium

I talked about trauma and post-traumatic growth in Chapter 11. Grief has a strange way of softening over time, reshaping itself into something that doesn't entirely disappear, but becomes a quiet companion. When Lou Lou passed away from cancer, the enormity of the loss felt like a tidal wave that would drown me. In those early days, I couldn't imagine thriving or finding beauty in the years of struggle. All I could do was survive each moment.

We had been partners in every sense of the word—her energy and positivity filled our home, her kindness stitched together the fabric of our lives. Watching cancer steal her from me was an excruciating process, and yet, even in her weakest moments, she remained a force of love and grace. She faced her illness with courage, constantly reminding me to look for the small joys—a soft sunset, a swim in the ocean, walking Benson, her dog, and the warmth of holding hands.

When she was gone, the absence was hard to bear. Purely focused on the kids, I stumbled through my days in a fog. I clung to her memory, replaying our moments like a fragile film reel. There was also some guilt to deal with: had I done enough, and had we made the right choices?

For a long time, I resisted the idea of moving forward, as though healing would somehow betray her memory. But slowly, imperceptibly, life began to seep back in. The kids' growth and increasing independence accelerated this process. As you rise through any form of trauma and are committed to self-discovery and care, you form a connection with your body and soul with a tremendous amount of self-awareness.

During these moments of connection and reflection, I began to understand the words of the poet Rainer Maria Rilke: "One day, in retrospect, the years of struggle will strike you as the most beautiful." Initially, I bristled at the idea. How could the years of anguish hold beauty? But as time passed, I realised that the struggle shaped me, just as a river carves through rock to form a canyon.

Through grief, I discovered resilience I didn't know I had. I learnt to cherish life's fleeting, precious nature and to savour the ordinary moments I once took for granted. The pain, though raw and jagged, forced me to grow, to become someone who could endure and also find meaning in the aftermath.

Today, I thrive not despite my loss, but because of it. Our love continues to guide me, infusing my life with a sense of purpose. I've committed to community work, I've extended my friendship circle, pursued passions I once set aside, and even found joy in the prospect of future love, ready to connect and build a romantic relationship with someone from organic beginnings.

The years of struggle, the sleepless nights, the tears, the aching loneliness have become a mosaic of memories, each piece adding depth to my life. They are beautiful because they were transformative, not because they were beautiful. They remind me that even in the darkest chapters, there is light to be found, and in the end, love is what endures.

Derren Brown's book *Happy: Why More or Less Everything is Absolutely Fine* is a comforting reminder of the inevitability of change. He astutely points out that to live without anxieties is to live without growth. Few people find a better partner without first experiencing the pain of a break-up. We don't change our careers without first letting our current job get us down; we don't start anything new without the pain of ending the old or the frustration of enduring it. Disturbance can signal that we are moving in the right direction—out of our comfort zone. To remain tranquil and comfortable would deny us the opportunity for growth. To remain happy would stop us from flourishing. We can manage our anxiety in the ways we've discussed, but when it stirs, it is likely to be a helpful signal from an unintended part of us that now wishes to be heard. Rather than seek to expunge all sadness, we might know when to pay attention to what it offers.

It was during an emotional lull in July 2024 that all my positive momentum shifted due to a relationship issue. I wrote on my blog in August:

> … after multiple months of flourishing, I would be negligent to think there would be no dips on the horizon to navigate.
>
> I understand that being happy every day is inherently improbable due to the dynamic nature of human experiences, emotional variability and external circumstances.
>
> Human emotions are inherently fluid and subject to change. The complexity of the human emotional spectrum makes it impossible to sustain a single emotional state, such as happiness, for an extended period. Emotions are not static; they ebb and flow in response to a plethora of factors. This variability is a fundamental

aspect of the human experience, enabling individuals to navigate diverse situations and adapt to shifting circumstances.

Life is full of challenges, setbacks and uncertainties that can disrupt our feelings of happiness. Personal losses, health issues, financial difficulties and interpersonal conflicts are common occurrences that can trigger negative emotions. These experiences are part of the human condition and contribute to the rich tapestry of emotional diversity. The inevitability of encountering difficult situations is a regular part of life, making the idea of perpetual happiness unrealistic. It's okay not to be okay all the time.

July was challenging for me, and I'm still on the journey to overcome this tough period. It's a process, and I'm learning to navigate the ups and downs of life with the wisdom I have acquired from previous experiences. Each challenge is an opportunity for growth, and I'm committed to emerging stronger from this difficult time.

I went on to map out my plan (it was like a mini version of the one I wrote when I was in a full-blown rut) to work my way out of the dip as quickly and effectively as possible.

I had a personal epiphany during my emotional dip. I had started writing this book with a sibling as the intended audience, but I soon realised I was writing equally for myself. Richard Bach aptly said, "We teach best what we most need to learn."

I leaned on my scaffolding, which was all of this book's chapters, and I managed the dip better than I would have without the wisdom I had gained and that formed the foundation of this book. Exploring and understanding happiness, discovering a philosophy and leaning on the ancient wisdom, always learning, being disciplined, and forever changing my habits.

As we near the final pages of this book, I refer to this part as "stitching it all together." But stitching only begins once you've chosen your thread. That first thread is simply about starting—laying something down, however small, and seeing what holds. You might only have 15 minutes a day, but that's enough. If something lifts your mood or brings clarity, you'll return to it. And when something becomes routine—ritual, even—it naturally makes space for the following thread. Before you realise it, you're layering small wins one on top of the other, and the compound effect begins to bloom.

At my lowest, the only way I could get moving in the morning was by hurling myself off the Balmoral Pier. What started as a Herculean effort is now the highlight of my day. That cold water plunge became my reset button. Similarly, after giving up alcohol for a year, I found something better than self-control—I found freedom. I could go out, laugh, connect, and return home completely clear, already excited to meet the sunrise with full presence.

Book in a handful of Pilates classes, and suddenly you've racked up hundreds. Getting up early feels impossible, until one day, it doesn't. And soon you're chasing the glow on the horizon, not the snooze button. Ditch Coca-Cola for a week and before long, even the idea of soda tastes artificial. One decision ripples into many: you drop sugar, ditch the processed junk, and unlock a clarity you didn't know was missing.

Even small changes, such as creating a pause between a trigger and your response, can give you a significant edge. It's not just about willpower—it's about widening the space between reaction and action so you can step in with awareness. With that awareness comes choice. And with that choice comes sovereignty over your thoughts, feelings and actions.

This is how the stitching happens—not all at once, but piece by piece. As you weave your habits, choices and values together, you'll begin to see the shape of something deeply personal and powerful: the authentic you, living in alignment with your purpose.

****

Let's stitch some key points together. Imagine giving yourself the rare gift of clarity—a whole year free from hangovers, guilt and second-guessing. Quitting alcohol for 12 months isn't a forever promise; it's a reset button for your body, mind and spirit. A quiet rebellion against numbing, and a return to feeling. Declare this month a clear-headed one. Just one. See how it feels when you wake up each day with nothing to regret and everything to gain.

Food is more than fuel—it's instruction for your cells, your mood, your energy. Every bite is either healing or harming. Wholefoods whisper vitality into your system, while processed ones dull the spark. The path to better health begins on your next plate. Add something vibrant and natural to your next meal—a burst of colour and life. Swap your soda for water or herbal tea. Cheers to that.

Your body is a beautiful machine built to move. Not just in gyms, but through daily life—walking, dancing, stretching, reaching. Every step is a thank you. Stop moving and the engine stiffens. Keep moving and it thrives. Step out the front door, walk the block and stretch under the sky. Five minutes of movement can awaken a whole day.

In the noise of the world, mindfulness is your quiet refuge. It doesn't ask for incense or silence—just your attention. It brings your scattered mind back to the present, where life is unfolding. Close your eyes. Inhale deeply. Exhale slowly. Let that breath anchor you. Did you feel that? That's presence.

Early mornings are sacred ground—still, undisturbed, yours. When the world is asleep, your soul can speak. These are the golden hours to plan, reflect, or be. Set your alarm for just 15 minutes earlier. Use those minutes to move slowly, sip something warm, and welcome the day on your terms.

The cracks in you aren't flaws—they're the places the light gets in. Growth after trauma is hard-earned, but it's also profound. Each time you rise, you do so with more truth, more tenderness, more grit. Think of something you've survived. Write down what it gave you, not just what it took.

The Stoics didn't preach detachment—they taught resilience. They knew that peace comes from focusing on what you can control and letting go of what you can't. It's calm in the chaos. Grace in the storm. Ask yourself, "Is this mine to control?" If the answer is no, release it.

You are not your past. Not your wounds. Not what they did. Holding on only keeps you stuck in stories that no longer serve you. Letting go is your permission slip to heal. Write down one burden you're ready to drop. Then close your eyes, take a breath, and let it go—even if just for today.

Purpose isn't a thunderclap, it's a whisper. It thrives in the small, sacred moments where your passions intersect with service. Following it makes life feel less like a to-do list and more like a calling. Ask yourself, "What matters to me?" Please write it down. Then do one small thing that aligns with it.

Think of your life as a patchwork: each habit a stitch, each moment a thread. No single one defines you, but together, they make something beautiful. This is your tapestry. Choose one thread today. Just one. Stitch it in with care and intention. The rest will follow.

*"No man is free who is not master of himself."* — *Epictetus.*

True freedom and flourishing begin with self-discipline—choosing what's good for you over what's easy. A structured wellness plan is a form of self-mastery, not self-denial. Wellness isn't a checklist—it's a tapestry. When you prioritise wellness in all its forms, you're not just ticking boxes for your physical health. You're weaving together threads of vitality, clarity, emotional depth, meaningful connection and personal purpose. Throughout the preceding chapters, we've explored how true wellness extends far beyond the gym or a green smoothie. It's a rich, layered approach to living that touches your body, mind, heart, relationships and spirit. When these dimensions align, happiness doesn't feel like a goal. It feels like a natural state of being.

Moving your body with purpose, fuelling it well and giving it proper rest recharges more than just your energy levels—it becomes the fuel for joy, focus and emotional steadiness. Meanwhile, your mind craves nourishment too—through curiosity, learning, mindfulness and calm. When your thoughts are clear and your mental space is respected, your entire life softens into a more harmonious rhythm.

Emotionally, tuning in to your inner world—welcoming your feelings instead of avoiding them—builds resilience and depth. Cultivating kind and healthy relationships, practising self-compassion and making space for emotional recovery is like building a sanctuary within yourself.

Then there's your soul, the quiet compass within. When you explore your values and sense of purpose, and reflect on feeling connected to something greater than yourself —whether that be nature, community, spirit, or legacy —you'll discover a richer form of fulfilment that goes deeper than happiness alone.

Do something simple, something we've spoken about. Try it today. Let this be the first stitch. Once the long-term benefits start to show—more energy, better moods, sharper focus, more profound calm—you won't need convincing to continue. You'll naturally adjust and refine your practice, creating a personalised blueprint that fits your life. If you fall off track, you'll remember how good it felt to care for your whole self, and that memory will help you return.

If you live with a partner, loop them in. Help them understand why you're making these changes—not to persuade them to follow, but to create alignment in the space you share. Wellness is harder to maintain when your environment works against it. Even better, invite them to walk beside you. Change is more powerful when it's shared. Find someone who will keep you accountable. Talk. Share. Celebrate the wins together. Feel the transformation not just in yourself, but between you.

And if you can, seek out a role model—someone already living a version of the life you aspire to. Their path won't be identical to yours, but it can light the way. Learn from their habits, mistakes, triumphs and values. Their lived wisdom can give you tools and shortcuts that save you from trial and error. Their presence can uplift your standards. Their encouragement can help you silence self-doubt and step into your potential more boldly.

A mentor doesn't just offer advice—they become a mirror for what's possible. Their belief in you can strengthen your self-confidence. And because they've travelled this road before, their insights will often reveal what books or podcasts can't: the hidden gears behind growth. They can challenge you to elevate not just what you do, but how you think, live and lead yourself.

Ultimately, surrounding yourself with supportive people—a friend, a partner, a mentor or a fellow seeker—can dramatically accelerate your journey. You're not meant to figure it all out alone. Stitch it together with what you've learnt, lean into what feels right, and live the wellness story that's uniquely yours.

You may have to go at this alone. If so, let that be a testament to your strength, not a limitation. Walking this path solo can be daunting, but it also offers profound rewards—self-trust, clarity and inner resilience. You'll learn to listen more closely to your own needs, tune into your intuition, and discover just how capable you are. Solitude can become a sacred space where transformation quietly unfolds. And though it may feel lonely at times, know this: every choice you make in service of your wellbeing is an act of self-respect, and that energy will ripple out. Eventually, the right people will see your light and either support your journey or be inspired to start their own. Keep going. You are becoming the role model someone else will one day need.

Make decisions today for your 90-year-old future self—the version of you who will thank you for every nourishing meal, every walk in the sunshine, every boundary you honoured, and every quiet moment you carved out for rest and reflection. A life of wellness isn't about perfection; it's about small, steady choices that add up to something extraordinary. You won't always get it right, but showing up for yourself over and over again is the most loving thing you can do. Let your life be a gentle unfolding, guided by the question: "Will this choice help me thrive in the long run?" Because that 90-year-old is you. They're cheering you on right now.

## REMEMBER THIS

"First say to yourself what you would be and then do what you have to do," urged Epictetus, reminding us that all meaningful change begins with clarity and intention. A wellness intention and plan is not just a checklist of habits, but a declaration of who you want to become. It's a compass that aligns your daily choices with your highest values. As Zeno of Citium taught, wellbeing is built "little by little", yet it becomes no small thing. Every mindful step you take—each healthy meal, restful night, deep breath or morning walk—compounds into something extraordinary. This is your beginning. Start small. Start with purpose. But above all—start now.

# CONCLUSION

*If you don't design your own life plan,
chances are you'll fall into someone else's plan.
And guess what they have planned for you? Not much.*
— Jim Rohn

After reading all the preceding chapters, it might seem like I'm doing a lot for my wellness—and I am. But this isn't the result of a sudden transformation. It's the product of years of small, intentional steps, layered one on top of the other. Each wellness practice started as a seed, planted with purpose and nurtured with discipline. In the beginning, it was effort that carried me forward. But with time, those efforts wove themselves into the fabric of my daily life. What once took willpower now feels as natural as breathing. That's the real magic: when consistency meets patience, the impossible begins to feel inevitable. Progress doesn't demand perfection—just the courage to keep going, one step at a time.

I love this advice by Gandhi: "Keep your thoughts positive, because your thoughts become your words. Keep your words positive, because your words become your behaviour. Keep your behaviour positive, because your behaviour becomes your habits. Keep your habits positive, because your habits become your values. Keep your values positive, because your values become your destiny."

Evidence suggests that I, like everyone else, have a baseline—or what some call a "set point"—of happiness. From what I've seen in others and felt in myself, we're all born with different emotional thermostats. Some people seem naturally sunnier, while others carry a heavier sky. Genetics plays a role, no doubt. I feel I am an individual who has to try a little harder, as my thermostat may be below the mean. Regardless of what life throws at us—promotions, setbacks, heartbreaks, windfalls—we tend to drift back towards our average. The highs are exhilarating and the lows can be crushing, but the research is clear: we usually return to where we started. We bounce, we wobble, but over time, we settle.

But here's what I've come to believe through experience—life events alone won't permanently raise that baseline. Not in a lasting, soul-deep way. What will is a deliberate, sustained commitment to wellness. It took me over two decades of adulthood to figure that out. And when I finally did, it hit me hard: no one is coming to do this for me. I am the architect of my happiness. If I want long-term change, I have to take full ownership of my physical, mental and spiritual evolution.

Improving my baseline happiness hasn't been about chasing peak moments or living in constant euphoria. It's been about building something more grounded—something made of balance, meaning and connection. And for me, that shift started in the mind. Gratitude cracked the door open. Perspective widened it. Self-compassion softened the edges, and acceptance taught me where to let go. Staying curious keeps my thinking fresh. And having a clear sense of purpose gives each day a quiet hum of direction.

Let me be honest—I haven't invented anything new in these pages. I'm not offering breakthroughs. All I did was take old wisdom, tested through centuries, and live it. And when I did, things began to move. Subtly at first. A little more lightness here, a little more clarity there. I'm still early in the journey, and I know there are storms ahead I can't yet see. But when I glance back, I can already trace the turns that have lifted me.

Daily habits have been a game changer. Movement shifts my mood and sharpens my focus. Nature reminds me I'm part of something vast and alive. Restorative sleep and fuelling myself with real, whole foods have changed more than just my body. They've changed the way I feel about life. And one of the most pivotal shifts? Removing alcohol. It was clouding my clarity, dulling the edges of my potential. Letting it go brought me back into balance.

I've learnt that happiness doesn't grow in isolation—it blooms in connection. Honest conversations, small gestures of kindness and a sense of belonging have all helped ground me. The more I allow myself to be real, vulnerable, fully human, the more deeply I connect and the less alone I feel.

Growth has been the final thread. I read to expand my mind. I learn to stretch my comfort zone. Discipline gives me the scaffolding to stay upright when motivation fades. And when I lose myself in creative flow—whether through writing, movement, or stillness—I remember what it feels like to be fully alive. My anchor through all of this has been a spiritual and philosophical practice: Stoicism, mindfulness and letting go. These aren't rigid rituals—they're my compass when the world feels chaotic.

None of these changes have brought fleeting highs. They've built something quieter, steadier, and far more valuable—a higher baseline. A version of happiness that holds steady through the winds of life. One that lets me stand tall, grounded in who I am, and fully present in the life I'm creating.

Consider what you would tell your kids if you only had a few weeks to live. What wisdom would you want to pass on? What values would you emphasise? What regrets would you urge them to avoid? What vices would you wish didn't control them? Maybe you'd tell them to be kind, to take risks, to forgive quickly, to love deeply, or to live with integrity and courage. You might remind them that time is precious, that relationships matter more than possessions, and that their worth isn't tied to success or failure.

Now ask yourself—are you living that advice? Are you modelling the very things you'd want them to carry forward when you're gone? If not, why not start now? The truth is we don't always get to choose how much time we have left. But we do get to choose how we live today.

Live like it matters. Every day is a new chance to build a better, wiser, stronger version of yourself. Keep learning—because wisdom isn't something you arrive at, it's something you build, choice by choice, day by day.

Make gratitude a daily habit. Not just when life feels good, but especially when it doesn't. Gratitude shifts your focus from what's lacking to what's already abundant—and that shift can change everything.

In every interaction, strive to be the best human you can be. Lead with kindness, patience and integrity. You never know the impact a single moment of presence or compassion can have on someone else's life.

Focus only on what you can control—your effort, your attitude, your response. Let go of what you can't. This is where peace lives.

Step back from your thoughts. Observe them without judgement. You are not your thoughts. You are the awareness behind them, and in that awareness, you'll find clarity and calm.

When negative emotions rise, don't suppress, escape or explode. Sit with them. Let them move through you. Surrendering pain consciously transforms it—resisting it only prolongs it.

Start caring for your body like it's the only one you get—because it is. Stop buying ultra-processed foods. Build the discipline to avoid sugar. Fuel your body, don't numb it.

Lift weights. Get strong—physically and mentally. Strength builds confidence, and confidence builds momentum.

Breathe. Become aware of it. Return to it. Your breath is your anchor in chaos, your pause in the noise.

Go to bed a little earlier. Wake at the same time every day. Rest is not a reward—it's a requirement. Your body and brain need it to rebuild, recharge and thrive.

And above all, do more of what brings meaning to your life. Don't wait for permission. Live in alignment with what matters most to you. That's where purpose lives.

## REMEMBER THIS

I don't expect you to follow exactly what I have done, but I do hope you've already made a start. If you have taken a moment to reflect on how to build your scaffolding for a better, more intentional life, then I consider that a win. As the ancient Chinese proverb goes, the best time to plant a tree was 20 years ago; the second-best time is now. Your path will be your own, as it should be. But begin. The smallest steps taken today—towards better choices, kinder thoughts, and deeper awareness—can quietly transform your entire foundation. Don't wait for perfect. Start building a life that feels honest, rich, and deeply yours. That's the kind of happiness worth growing.

# ACKNOWLEDGEMENTS

To my beautiful wife, Louise: You understood me more deeply than anyone and always let me be unapologetically myself.

Lou often spoke of "her village"—the family and friends who supported her through every high and low. That community made it possible for Lou and our family to spend those precious, challenging months in Germany, pursuing every treatment option available. Those were some of the hardest and most meaningful days of our lives, and they were only possible because of the people who stood beside her.

To my mates: Lifelong friends are the anchors of our journey—reminders of who we've been, witnesses to who we're becoming, and proof that love and loyalty can outlast time itself.

Mum and Dad, with five kids often pulling you in five different directions, you've somehow been there for each of us every step of the way—steady, selfless, and full of love. You are the quiet strength that has held our family together through every season of life.

Grandma and Grandpa, Noah and Evie adore their time with you. Your support makes my life easier to manage, and you bring warmth, wisdom, and a sense of home that wraps around them like a gentle embrace.

To all of Noah's and Evie's aunts, uncles, and cousins—but especially Elysia, Jon, Joshua, Sadie, Billie, and Georgie—thank you for being ever-present, geographically, physically, and emotionally.

You have been a constant pillar of strength for Lou's precious babies.

To Jessica, Grace and the growing team at Hembury Books, thank you for a seamless publishing collaboration and for making the journey of bringing this book to readers around the world so enjoyable and rewarding.

To Zeno of Citium and all the Stoics, thank you for shaping a philosophy that continues to illuminate the path toward clarity, resilience, and peace—making life not only easier, but richer in meaning.

To David R. Hawkins, thank you for your profound insights into the power of letting go. Your work has helped countless souls, including mine, find freedom in surrender and strength in acceptance.

To my siblings: I love you. Let's set an intention to all be there for each other, for the rest of our lives. To Alisha, thank you for being the first reader of this book, for embracing every suggestion with an open heart, and for gaining so much from it that it gave me the confidence to share it with the world.

www.ingramcontent.com/pod-product-compliance
Lightning Source LLC
Chambersburg PA
CBHW020109240426
43661CB00002B/84